MW00625033

Affirm Your Self

DAY · BY · DAY

Seed Thoughts For Loving Your Self

Suzanne E. Harrill, M.Ed.

AFFIRM
YOUR SELF
Day By Day

Innerworks Publishing
P. O Box 270865
Houston, Texas 77277-0865

http://ourworld.compuserve.
com/homepages/innerworks

First Printing Cover Design by Diane Wilkinson
ORIGINAL ISBN: 0-9625996-1-1
Cover Design and Logo by Susan Pietrowski
Utopian Art 713/662-0561
ISBN 1-883648-22-X

Dedication

This book is dedicated to the beauty, love,
and truth of your True Self and to every
member of humanity.

Suzanne Harrill

Passages for your Birthday, Your Mother's or
Father's Birthday can be found on
September 7, January 31, and August 31
respectively. Please substitute the actual
dates these birthdays occur in your life.

Acknowledgments

Creating this book was a group experience. I am grateful to my friends who helped and supported me. Thank you to B.J. Callihan, Kevin Kauffman, Diane Langley, Carol Estes, Sylvia Salinas, Jo Strauss, Beverly Threadgill, and Diane Wilkinson. A special thank you to Susan Pietrowski for the art work for this new edition.

My very special thanks to Diane Langley, whose love and support enabled me to write this book. Without her labor of love, I could not have created such a finished piece of work.

Exceptions to the Copyright agreement: Anyone who shares information in this book for teaching purposes or for personal growth has my permission to copy small portions of this book.

Please give credit to the author and give freely to others the Harrill Self-Esteem Indicator and the Twelve Steps of Building Self-Esteem.

A Letter

Dear Suzanne:
As I read these passages all those persons in me became conscious. The mother, the father, and the inner-child in me came to surface. We came together as we had never been before. We were a family unit within me and we read and shared as a union of souls.

My usual means of assimilating information was no longer sufficient. I felt compelled to absorb more than I was capable of internalizing. Answers to questions seemed to bounce off the page at me. I became controlled by an impulse that hungered for more and more information. My inner-self persuaded me to read on and on, and over and over again until the words and I became intimately connected.

You have honored me by sharing so much of yourself with me. I want to thank you for the experience. I have learned so much from you. Your insights into the human consciousness are far beyond printed words on a page. You are truly the essence of humanity. I am more for having read this.   *Sylvia*

Foreword

"Everyday is a new beginning." We smile at such a cliche not realizing the profound significance of the pure truth it contains, for through the darkness of night the old passes away and the light of dawn signifies a new day and a new life—if we capitalize on the opportunity.

An ancient teaching says that the beginning thought upon awakening sets the tone for the rest of the day. Considering this I was reminded of once watching and listening to a quartet preparing to sing. The leader hummed a note, a tone, and the others caught it and enthusiastically plunged into song on the same key, at the right pitch. They took advantage of a new beginning and issued forth a chorus of success—because they were in tune with the universal principle of harmony.

That's what this book is all about—getting a jump-start with the proper tone and pitch and continuing in the right rhythm throughout the day. Ralph Waldo Emerson wrote, "We are what we think about all day long...the good mind is known by the choice of what is positive, of what is advancing. We must embrace the affirmative." What do most of us think about all day long? Usually what we do not want rather than what we do, and the primary reason for this is a sense of unworthiness. We have forgotten who we are—the highest of creation and the completeness of the universe—heirs to all that which is good, true and beautiful. But with forgetting also comes remembering—a change of mind—and we have the power to choose that which is positive, of what is advancing. Day by day we can etch deeply in consciousness the truth of our being and transform our self-image and self-esteem, becoming new creatures on the side of life where wonders never cease.

The word "consciousness" is an enigma to many people, yet it is nothing more than the awareness, understanding and knowledge of our identity. And as this self-image expands to encompass our Spiritual Self, the attributes of that Self begin to be reflected in the phenomenal world and miracles become the order of the day. Just ask Suzanne Harrill. Suzanne is one of those practical Professional Counselors who blends intellectual expertise and spiritual understanding with the meaningful personal experiences of life. The result, or end-product, is a model for consciousness expansion—to help us realize our power through a deeper awareness, understanding and knowledge of who and what we truly are.

In *AFFIRM YOUR SELF Day by Day*, she takes us on a full year's course of New Beginnings—with delightful seed thoughts to plant in the garden of mind to change the way we think, to change our beliefs, thus changing our lives. Assume the role of the gardener and follow Suzanne's recommended sowing sequence. Let your mind be cultivated daily and water the seeds with fertile expectations, making sure that the weeds of trouble and discontent are continually uprooted. Do your part with dedication and enthusiasm, and a rich and bountiful harvest will be yours.

John Randolph Price
Author of SUPER BEINGS,
ANGEL ENERGY and THE ANGELS WITHIN US
Cofounder of the Quartus Foundation
See December 31 for more information.

Introduction

This is a daily guide to help you learn to
love and accept yourself. It will help you
learn new patterns of thinking and
feeling. When you learn to mature your
fear thoughts and beliefs into love
thoughts and beliefs, you experience a
shift in how you feel. Wherever you are
on your journey of self-discovery, use this
daily guide to help you build a loving
relationship with your Self.

  Some of you are planting new seed
thoughts that will take time to root and
grow. Others may be further along and may
use this guide as a reminder to stay on
track. The concepts presented in this book
build upon each other. If you begin using
this book on any day of the year other than
January 1, it may be necessary to

backtrack a few days or a month to help the passage make sense.

A theme in this book is building self-esteem which is how you feel about yourself. Sound self-esteem is a place of feeling comfortable being who you are, your true Spiritual Self. When you allow your Spiritual Self to love you without conditions, you feel worthy, full of love, and able to pass it on to others.

You may want to take the Harrill Self-Esteem Indicator on the next page before you begin this book and then repeat the Indicator periodically to gauge your progress.

Many people have learned to open spiritually through the Twelve Step Programs. I have rewritten the Twelve Steps of Alcoholics Anonymous in holistic, present tense for those who would benefit from this approach for building self-esteem and loving yourself. It follows the Harrill Self-Esteem Indicator.

I would also like to encourage you to expand the love in your life to others by placing the name of a loved one, a friend, or a special person on the page corresponding to the day of their birth. You will then be able to include them in your focus for that day. The love in which you are living and growing will then radiate to all those within your world.

*Namasté,

Suzanne

*I honor the place in you of light, and love, and truth, and beauty. When you are in that place in you and I am in that place in me, there is only one of us.

The Harrill Self-Esteem
Awareness Indicator

Rate yourself on a scale of 0 to 4 based upon
your current feelings and behaviors:

0=   I **never** feel or behave that way.
1=   I **rarely** feel or behave that way.
        (25% of the time)
2=   I **sometimes** feel or behave that way.
        (50% of the time)
3=   I **usually** feel or behave that way.
        (75% of the time)
4=   I **always** feel or behave that way.
        (100% if the time)

Self Esteem Statements

_____1. 1 accept myself the way I am right
        now. I like being who I am, even as I
        grow and evolve.
_____2. I am worthy, simply because I am
        alive. I do not have to earn my
        worthiness.
_____3. I get my needs met before I meet the
        needs of others (exception young
        children).
_____4. I do not let it bother me when other
        people blame or criticize me.

_____ 5. I always tell myself the truth about what I am feeling.

_____ 6. I do not compare myself with other people.

_____ 7. I feel of equal value to other people regardless of my performance, looks, I.Q., achievements, or possession (or lack of them).

_____ 8. I take responsibility for my feelings and emotions. I do not blame others when I am upset, angry, or hurt.

_____ 9. I learn from my mistakes rather than use them to confirm my unworthiness.

_____ 10. I separate my behavior from my inner self, or spiritual essence.

_____ 11. I understand that I can choose to love each human being without having an active relationship with them.

_____ 12. I accept other people as they are, even when they do not meet my expectations or if I dislike their behaviors or beliefs.

_____ 13. I release responsibility for anyone else's actions, needs, thoughts, moods or feelings, I am only responsible for my own (exception...your children when they are young).

____14. I feel my own feelings and think my own thoughts, even when those around me think or feel differently.

____15. I am kind to myself and stop using "shoulds" and "oughts" to put myself down with value-judging comments.

____16. I allow others to have their own interpretation and experience of me.

____17. I look for something positive in each individual I meet.

____18. I forgive myself and others for making mistakes and being un-aware.

____19. I accept responsibility for my interpretation of other people's behavior and my response to them. I stop projecting my shadow onto others.

____20. I do not dominate others or allow others to dominate me.

____21. I am my own authority. I make decisions that are in my own and others' best interests.

____22. I develop and use my talents.

____23. I balance giving and receiving in my life. I have good boundaries with others.

____24. I am responsible for changing what I do not like in my life.
____25. I choose to love and respect every human being, including myself.

This is not a test and does not tell you your level of self-esteem. It simply gives feedback on areas of your belief system, behavior and feelings that relate to self-esteem. By working on the low ones you can improve how you feel about yourself.

These 25 statements are healing affirmations. You might want to write the low ones on 3x5 cards for emphasis and review them often.

About the Twelve Steps

I have rewritten the Twelve Steps of Alcoholics Anonymous for people working on the universal need to love and support themselves.

Many people who read the original Twelve Steps have a problem stating "I am powerless." Those people who practice reprogramming their subconscious mind through positive affirmation do not believe in stating a negative such as this.

I find it helpful to talk about the self in two parts: the little self (ego, conditioned self, or personality self) and the Greater Self (Spiritual Self, Transpersonal Self, or Higher Self). In reality there is no split; they are one. Until a person experiences this oneness, however, it seems as if there is a separation or split.

The Twelve Steps of Building Self-Esteem address this split. By practicing this process of healing through these Twelve Steps, one is capable of experiencing the truth which is wholeness.

The Twelve Steps move a person from the powerless state of consciousness of the little self to an empowered Spiritually Awakened Being. The personality self is created from the past and is subject to addiction, pain, illusion, and fear. The experiences of childhood conditioned the personality. Since most parenting was not totally adequate (no blame implied), the personality self is stuck wanting what it did not get in the past. This focus on the past of pain, deprivation, etc. creates the split from the Higher Self. The Twelve Steps help you on the spiritual journey of knowing who you are, a Spiritual Being having a physical experience.

The Twelve Steps of Building Self-Esteem

(Adapted from the Twelve Steps
of Alcoholics Anonymous)

1. I admit my little self (ego) is powerless to control my negative thoughts and feelings—-my life of feeling unworthy is not working and is unmanageable.

2. I believe my wholeness depends on experiencing Love from God as I understand God (Higher Self, God Within).

3. I choose to turn my life over to the care and direction of my Higher Self (God Within) to become fully conscious,a self-actualized being.

4. I continue to know myself, looking at all past behavior, guiding beliefs, and feelings that have manifested negatively in my life.

5. I admit and forgive myself for fearful thoughts, words, and actions that block Love in my life.

6. I am ready to transform all aspects of myself that block the power of Love in my life.

7. I humbly ask my Higher Self (God Within) to achieve this transformation.

8. I make a list of all the situations and people whom I believe I have hurt or whom I feel have hurt me, because of unawareness. I am willing to make peace with my past.

9. I heal these relationships directly unless it does not support the highest good.

10. I continue to expand my awareness and heal negative patterns that I see. I admit my mistakes openly and take responsibility for my life.

11. I consciously experience more and more Love from my Higher Self through prayer, meditation, and contemplation. I chose to consciously express this Divine Love through me.

12. I am an awakening spiritual being as a result of practicing these steps. I continue to practice these principles and to love myself and others. I share this love with others who choose my assistance.

These Twelve Steps were rewritten by Suzanne E. Harrill, M.Ed., L.P.C. (713)661-8284

What is Sound Self-Esteem?

A feeling of total acceptance
and love for yourself as you are.
A quiet comfortable place of enjoying
being who you really are:
your True Self.
When you live being who you really are,
you feel good and want to
actualize your life.

What is High Self-Esteem?

- Having an internal locus of control, getting okayness from within.
- Ability to balance extremes within self.
- Learning from mistakes and being able to say, "I made a mistake, I'm sorry."
- Taking responsibility for own perceptions, reactions and not projecting onto others.
- Ability to listen to inner self and act on this guidance.
- Having self-respect, self-confidence, and self-acceptance.
- Having awareness of strengths and weekness.
- Knowing areas of self to be improved, what needs to be accepted.
- Growing in awareness and taking positive risks.

New Beginnings

It's a brand new year.
Today, I have a new beginning, a fresh
   new start.
I let go of yesterday's fears and take a
   step forward on my path.
As I focus on this present day, I choose
   to love and support myself.
I release old negative patterns, and I
   live fully in this day.
I find my way back to my life path if I
   have been diverted.
I commit to discovering and being
   exactly who I am.

I love the being that is me.

Potential Self

I am like an acorn growing into my Full-Potential Self.

At each place along my life path I am a perfect expression of this Self.

I am being exactly what I am capable of being at each moment; this is dependent upon my degree of awareness.

As I grow in awareness, I do better and better expressing the real me.

As it is never too late for the mighty oak tree to grow new branches, it is never too late for me to grow in confidence and security in being my true Self or to develop my interests and talents.

I am growing into my potential.

Worthiness

I cannot earn being worthy of love and
  acceptance.
It is my birthright.
Nothing I do, say, or think can change
  this truth.
I am a unique expression of the Higher
  Power.
I am worthy and of value regardless of
  whether I have accepted this or not.
Today, I choose to believe I am of
  value and am an important part of
  life.
Eventually, I will feel worthy.

I am worthy because I exist.

Self-Acceptance

To feel good about myself, it is
  important to accept myself the way I am
  right now.
If I put conditions on my self-
  acceptance, I miss the opportunity
  today to feel good.
Wanting something begins the creative
  process.
I may want to improve my communication
  skills, exercise more, finish school, get
  married, or be farther along in creating a
  life that I want.
Today is my place of power; I am learning
  to love and accept myself and am
  beginning to create the life I desire.

I accept myself right now, today.

Unconditional Love

I no longer expect anyone else to love me
   unconditionally.
If I turn my power over to others by relying
   on them for my good feelings, then I am
   bounced around by their moods and
   their ability to love.
When I turn within and connect with my
   Inner Self, a direct link to the Higher
   Power, I learn to love myself.
Today, when I feel lonely, unworthy,
   separate from others, and in need of
   love, I will turn inward and ask my Inner
   Self for this love without conditions.
I remember the truth that I cannot earn
   love, as it is already available as my
   birthright.

I unconditionally love myself.

Nurturing

I look for ways to nurture myself.
I realize that the unmet dependency needs
of my inner child require attention from
me.
When I am filled with love, people are then
attracted to my wholeness.
I visualize my inner child being filled with
love and affection from my adult self.
I sit or walk in nature and become very still
in order to feel my oneness with the
earth, plants, trees, and sky.
I take time to listen and respond to my inner
needs.

I do one thing today that nurtures me.

Responsibility

Only I have the power to create my life the
    way I want it.
I do not blame or give credit to anyone for
    who and what I am today.
Though people and events have interacted
    with me and influenced me, today I
    become a detective searching to
    understand what motivates me to think,
    feel, and act as I do.
I choose to work on my awareness and to
    take the risks necessary that will change
    my life and allow me to become more
    and more an expression of my True Self.

I am responsible for my own life.

Authority

I take responsibility for my choices.
Not making a choice, I realize, is a choice.
I willingly pay the consequences, both
  good and bad, for these choices.
I know I am in the "school of life" and learn
  from everything I do.
I no longer turn my power over to others to
  make my choices because I now am
  aware that I pay the consequences of
  their choices for me.
By making my own choices and taking
  responsibility for them, I become my own
  authority.

I am my own authority.

Going Within

I go within to feel good. I no longer
   evaluate my self-worth on outer
   appearances.
My value is not dependent on my
   achievements (or lack of them), what
   others expect of me, my physical beauty,
   the color of my hair or skin, my car, or the
   cost of my clothing.
The outer me creatively expresses how I
   think and feel on the inside of me.
Eventually, my inner beauty will shine.

*I allow my outer self to be a reflection of
my inner beauty and light.*

Inner Self

I listen to my Inner Self.
To build sound self-esteem, I get in touch
    with my inner needs today.
I know not to base my good feelings (or
    bad ones) on outer appearances,
    people, or circumstances.
I take a few moments, right now, to close
    my eyes and go inward.
I go to my place of peace and ask what I
    need today to feel more balanced in
    order to take the next step in expanding
    my awareness.
Do I need more activity or less?
Do I need to work on my physical,
    emotional, mental, or spiritual well-being?

*I acknowledge and listen to the voice of
my Inner Self.*

Achieving

I let go of seeking approval and value
   through my achievements.
I now do things to express the creative
   power within me.
I let my achievements be a form of personal
   pleasure.
I accept the cycles of my life.
I am worthy even when I am just "being"
   and not accomplishing measurable
   things.
During these inward cycles, the seeds of
   new achievements are sprouting and
   taking root.

*I enjoy creative power by using it to
achieve what is within me.*

Comparison

Today, I choose not to compare myself with anyone else.
This builds my self-esteem.
There is no longer a race to win.
I am a winner whether someone is ahead of me or behind me on the journey of life.
No one is better than or less than I am.
I no longer need to concern myself with how much progress I am making by looking at others.
I have a special assignment that only I can fulfill and that is to be "Me."
I have my own internal time schedule.

I stop comparing myself to others.

Conscious Awareness

Today, I look at my awareness.
I want to consciously know the things that
have been hidden from my view.
My awareness is everything that has
brought me to this present moment —
my genetic code, family patterns,
behavioral tendencies, every experience
that has ever happened to me, and
everything I am taking in with my six
senses.
As I look at myself, I discover more and
more of what has been unconscious
to me.

*I discover more and more who I am by
becoming consciously aware.*

Free-Will Choice

As I become more and more aware of my
inner needs, wishes, and values as
opposed to what other people want for
me, I make wiser choices.
I have greater free-will choice when I know
my Inner Self.
Today, I support myself by making choices
from this place of power.

*I expand my understanding of myself so
I have greater free-will choice.*

Past Pain

I release the pain of my past.

I no longer allow a difficult childhood, a marriage, or a negative-feeling experience to cripple the present day.

I see with detachment what took place in my past.

In order not to repeat patterns, I remember what happened.

I allow any hidden emotions to surface so that I can grieve; then I focus my mind in the present and see what is good and what is working.

I am healing the pain and fear from my past.

Emotional Reactions

I am becoming aware that my emotional reactions are bigger than the people or events that trigger these emotional reactions.

I am usually reacting to a pattern built up in my mind from many similar hurtful issues from my past.

Today, I am aware of my emotional reactions and ask myself questions such as, "Is this a pattern?" or "Has this response happened in me before?" or "What were the circumstances?" or "Of whom does this situation remind me?"

I choose to release myself from the emotional pain of the past by seeing the person or event as a trigger and not the cause of my upset feelings.

I allow people and events to "trigger" me in order to make peace with the past.

Value-Judging

Today, I stop finding fault with myself and
    others.
Rather than criticize or judge, I pay
    attention whenever I think I "should" or
    "ought" to do something differently.
These value-judgments lower my
    self-esteem.
To become more aware, I ask myself,
    "What am I willing to do, or not do, in the
    future if this situation comes up again?"
Then I live with the consequences of this
    choice.

I stop value-judging myself and others.

Mistakes

I am okay when I make a mistake; that is
 how I learn and grow.
If I had known the outcome of a choice
 before I made it, then I would have had
 the awareness to choose differently.
When I go over and over what I judge as
 bad or wrong, I lower my self-esteem.
I forgive myself for an unwise choice.
I learn from all mistakes which is the purpose
 behind the experience.

*I am accepting of myself when I make
a mistake.*

Feelings

My feelings are not right or wrong.
They are simply an inner guidance system
    giving me feedback on what my
    reactions are to everything going on in
    my daily experiences.
I am learning to put words to what I am
    feeling.
Once I do this, I can use my mind to make
    changes that will benefit me.
I listen to my feelings.

I accept and allow myself to feel.

Emotional Victim

Today, I give up being an emotional victim
by seeing the part I play in the drama.
I must turn inward to receive strength from
the Higher Power.
I begin by releasing unrealistic
expectations.
I accept people and events that I cannot
change.
I can only work on myself.
As I change, I no longer play my role as a
victim.

I give up being an emotional victim.

Behavior

I choose to understand my unwanted
behavior.

Today, I look behind my behavior to what
the causes are.

All behavior makes sense if I look at my
needs and the choices I make to get
them met.

Some of my needs are unconscious to me.

This is where I will focus to get some clarity
on why I do things I do not consciously
want to do.

I go within and ask my Inner Self for
thoughts, pictures, or feelings that give
me clues to this puzzle.

I am patient with the process of expanding
my awareness.

---

*All my behavior makes sense, so I am
easy on myself.*

Forgiveness

I forgive myself for things I have said, thought, or done in the past that I do not like.

I remind myself that I only did what I could do at that place in time, with the level of understanding I had.

It no longer serves me to use today's awareness to judge yesterday's actions.

Today, I know I would do it differently.

I have learned from my choices, even though they might have seemed to be mistakes.

I forgive myself for unaware things I have said and done in the past.

Giving

I fill myself today so that I can respond
    appropriately to the needs of others.
I stay conscious of what my needs are so
    that my boundaries are respected.
When I forget to work on myself, I give to
    others so that I will receive.
This is an inappropriate way to give.
Unattached giving requires me to be filled
    up and to give from my overflow.

**I fulfill my needs so that I can give
unconditionally to others.**

Awareness

My present level of awareness determines
what I am capable of doing at each
moment.
Therefore, I am always doing my best.
I need to go easy on myself and be
forgiving when I cannot do what I think I
should do.
This is especially difficult to understand if I
am not able to repeat a behavior or
level of achievement.
My best includes all aspects of myself—-
physical, emotional, mental, and spiritual.
When one part of me is out of balance, it
affects the rest of me.

*I am doing my best at each moment
with my present level of awareness.*

Blame

It serves no purpose for me to blame myself
or another for anything.

Blaming myself lowers my self-esteem. I am,
however, responsible for everything I say,
think, and do.

I learn from all consequences.

The negative consequences teach me to
make more aware choices.

Today, I notice when I have a habit of
punishing myself through blame.

I release this pattern.

When blame comes up, I ask myself
questions such as, "What expectations or
demands did I have that were not met?"
or "What can I learn from this situation
that will enable me to have a different
outcome next time?"

*I stop blaming myself for undesirable
actions, thoughts, and feelings.*

Forgiveness

I release myself from anything or anyone
   that I believe has hurt me.
I forgive people, situations, and myself for
   being unaware and causing me pain.
When I am ready, I detach and see us all as
   characters in a play acting out parts in a
   script that was written at an unconscious
   level of awareness.
I see that the victims, as well as the
   victimizers, were trapped, not realizing
   that they had conscious choices.
Today, I am more aware and choose to
   forgive so I can move beyond this script.
If this is a new idea for me, I may need time
   to get past my anger, denial, and/or grief.

*I forgive every person, including myself,
for being unaware and causing me pain.*

Preferences

Today, I work on my awareness of areas where I allow myself to be hurt and disappointed by having expectations that are too high.

When I demand a certain emotional outcome, this demand is an emotional addiction.

It helps me to have a preference for a certain outcome rather than an addiction.

Preferences are soft and flexible; demands are hard and rigid.

Preferences allow me to flow around what cannot be changed.

I turn my emotional demands into preferences.

Goals

Today, I will think about my goals.
I set realistic goals in the proper time frame
    for me.
I need to evaluate, prioritize, and adjust
    these goals periodically.
Standards set too low or too high lower my
    good feelings about myself.
I use only myself as the standard of
    measure.
As I grow and change, these goals may
    change.

*I set realistic goals and expectations
for myself.*

Thoughts and Feelings

Today, I work on identifying my feelings with
   words.
Every feeling has a thought behind it.
These can be grouped into two main
   categories: love and fear.
I am getting better and better at
   recognizing my love thoughts and
   allowing myself to feel them.
I also listen to my fear thoughts so that I will
   be aware of them.
I pull unhealthy seed thoughts planted in
   the garden of my consciousness.
I am responsible for replanting seed
   thoughts based upon love.

*I plant loving thoughts in the garden of
my mind.*

Boundaries

I pay attention to my boundaries.
I notice when I feel uncomfortable during
my interactions with others.
If I do feel uncomfortable, I will take care of
myself by making changes that support
me.
I may need to communicate to another or
simply stay conscious so that I do not
agree to anything that does not feel right
to me.
It is okay to say "no."
Some experiences are not healthy for me.

I set appropriate boundaries for myself.

My Mother

I love and appreciate my mother.
I am grateful for the gift of life she gave me
and the sacrifices she made for me.
All that I learned being her child is a part of
me now.
I release and forgive all the judgments and
criticisms I have about wanting things to
have been different in my childhood.
My inner mother loves and nurtures me.

(This passage may be read on your
mother's birthday.)

I love and appreciate my mother.

Others' Approval

It is okay if some people do not like me.
As I become more and more my real Self, I
   become less dependent on the approval
   of others for my well-being.
Some people will never like me, and I
   accept this.
I choose to love myself.
The choices I make regarding my behavior,
   wants, and needs are no longer based
   on the approval of others.

*I let go of expecting everyone to like
and support me.*

Giving

Today I focus on unconditional giving.
First, I fill myself emotionally and get my
  needs met; then I can give without an
  expectation of a return.
I listen to my Inner Self to identify what I
  need.
I meet these needs first so that my giving
  comes from the good feeling I get when
  expressing kindness towards another.

*I give love to the degree that
I am filled up.*

Receiving

I allow myself to receive.

When another person gives me a compliment or does a kindness for me, I accept the gift.

It is no longer something to be made light of, but rather, to be enjoyed and appreciated.

Giving and receiving are different halves of a whole.

One without the other is incomplete.

I receive graciously.

Behavior

I continue to detach from feelings of
worthiness that are based on my
behavior.
I realize that my behavior is predictable as
that is how I learned to get my needs
met.
To change behavior that I do not like, I first
determine my needs and then I look at
healthy ways to get those needs met.
I may want to observe people who are able
to get their needs met in a positive way;
they can serve as role models for me.
Finally, I take risks to follow through with
these new choices until these choices
become automatic for me.

*I look at my needs today. I choose
positive ways to get my needs met.*

Authentic Intentions

My intentions are more important than other
people's perceptions of them.

Though some people may criticize even my
best intentions, I choose to communicate as genuinely and authentically as I
am able.

I always have the understanding and
support of the Higher Power when my
intentions are good.

*I communicate with an intention of
being authentic and genuine.*

Mirrors

Everyone is my mirror.
I would not see something in another if it
were not a part of me.
I remember that everyone is capable of
wise and unwise actions.
Instead of judging them as good or bad, I
seek to learn from everyone I meet.
I spend time with the people who reflect my
goodness, love, and beauty.

*I see reflections of aspects of myself in
other people because they are
my mirrors.*

Talents

I feel good about myself when I develop my
    talents and abilities.
My talents may or may not be
    achievements highly valued
    by society.
My gifts may be playing the piano, writing,
    taking care of plants, working with
    animals, playing sports, or having the
    patience to listen to others in need.
I go within and remember the things I like to
    do and what excites me about life.
It is time again to focus on my talents and
    gifts so I can express more of who and
    what I am.

I choose to develop and use my talents.

Higher Self

I am an expression of my Higher Self.
There is much more to me than my
    personality, behavior, and mind.
I am a spiritual being that exists beyond the
    physical level of awareness.
As I grow in awareness, I learn more about
    this Greater Self.
A am never alone.
A personal relationship with my Greater Self
    builds my love and acceptance for all of
    my.
My Higher Self is my Spiritual Self.

*I am an expression of my Higher
Self, my Spiritual Essence.*

Nourishment

The energy from Spirit is the only real source
of my strength and power.
Today, I fill myself with Love from my Higher
Self which is able to easily receive energy
from Spirit.
As I live this day, I imagine golden energy
from a ball of light above my head
pouring down into my physical form.
This energy flows in and around and
through me to nourish all the cells of my
body.
My emotional well-being is uplifted by this
nourishment from Spirit.

*I nourish myself with love and light
from my Higher Self.*

Purpose

I have a special purpose only I can fulfill.

No one else is exactly like I am, so only I can fulfill the destiny of being me.

As I learn and grow in consciousness, I become more and more aware of my spiritual purpose.

I begin with listening to the real Self on the inside of me and let that express through my human self.

I have the important role of learning to become my Self.

Higher Will

As I get to know my Inner Self, I receive
communication from the Higher Power.
I ask this Power what the higher will and
purpose is for me.
I do this through meditation, prayer, and
time spent thinking and pondering.
By first putting myself in a receiving mode, I
am open to receive communication
from Spirit which might come as a picture
or thoughts or, perhaps, I receive a
feeling and only sense my intuition at
work.

I align myself with the
Higher Will and Purpose.

School of Life

Today, I look at life as if it were a school.
I remember that I am here to learn and
grow and to become fully aware of who
and what I am.
The challenges that come my way are seen
as part of the curriculum that I signed up
for at the spiritual level of my being.
Rather than criticize, deny, or avoid my
problems, I see them as opportunities for
growth.

*I am in the school of life and learn from
every experience.*

Problems

I choose to see the problems in the drama
of my life as a chance to do things
differently.
When I do this, I see alternatives that are
not obvious.
As I gather information on the issue giving
me difficulty, I see that there are people
who have walked a similar path before
me who are available to be my
teachers.
My problems are no longer traps; they are a
means to become more aware.

*I open my mind and heart in order to
see my problems differently.*

Love

I choose to express love today.
I begin with myself.
I see myself from the eyes of my Full-
    Potential Self.
I extend this love and appreciation of
    myself from my Self to all others.
Today, I notice what I like about myself and
    all others.

***I love and appreciate myself from the
place of Spirit.***

Question

I remember to question new ideas that I
   read in books or hear from others.
Before blindly putting them into my
   consciousness, I like to think about and
   see their practical application.
I can then reprogram my subconscious
   mind by changing unhealthy guiding
   beliefs (rules by which I live my life) for
   new ones.
I like to think about and prove the validity of
   new ideas.

I question as I open my mind to new
points of view.

Love vs. Like

Today, I am aware of the difference
between loving and liking.
I can unconditionally love someone and
not like their behavior.
My like or dislike of someone is an emotional
response; unconditionally loving them is
a mental decision.
Unconditional love does not dictate any
behavior.
Sometimes the most loving thing for me to
do is to say, "no."

*I love everyone including the people
whose behavior I dislike.*

Intellectualizing

Today, I notice when I am "in my head"
and not participating in my life.
Once I have gathered information to help
me solve my dilemmas in life, I act on
that information.
Talking about and analyzing my problems
are good to a point, however, my growth
stops when I spend too much time
intellectualizing.
I now begin taking risks to apply what
I know.

To grow, I experience what I know.

Illness

I let go of judging myself and others when
there is physical illness.

Illness does not mean a failure in spiritual
growth.

I pay attention to the messages my body
gives me in the metaphor of illness,
aches, or pain.

As I crack the code of the metaphors, I
make positive changes to heal my
thoughts and feelings.

I also take care of myself on the physical
level.

*I listen when my body talks to me
through illness and pain.*

Peace

World peace begins with me.
Today, I practice loving and forgiving so
    that I can experience inner peace.
It is predictable that I will get my feelings
    hurt or want to defend myself when
    another pushes my emotional buttons.
In order to change my reactive behavior
    and feelings, I balance myself by
    choosing inner peace.
I do this by continually practicing thoughts
    of love and forgiveness.

I choose inner peace.

Fear

Fear no longer stops my progress.
Today, I notice when I let my fear stop me
from taking risks.
If I visualize negative results when I see one
of my goals, I stop and bring my mind
back to the present moment.
When I use my mind appropriately, I see the
goal and determine the next step for me
in the process.
I talk gently and firmly to myself with my self-
talk by affirming my ability to risk even
when there is fear.

*I feel my fear and take positive risks
anyway.*

Assimilating

Many times I have judged myself as failing
    to grow when I have reached a plateau.
Today, I remind myself that a lot takes place
    on these plateaus.
I am assimilating what I have learned.
I am always growing.

I accept the plateaus in my life.

Value

I am of equal value to every other living being.

Talents, abilities, interests, energy levels, and awareness vary between people.

These things are not proof of my worthiness or unworthiness.

Comparison to others no longer determines my self-esteem.

I am of equal value and importance to every other person.

Approval

I become aware of my security needs that are dependent upon other people's approval.

As I learn new values, attitudes, beliefs, and behaviors, I do not expect others to always understand or be able to give me their approval.

It is important to allow others to disagree with me.

As I learn to love and support myself, I will not need approval or agreement from others to change my life.

I release the need for the approval of others in order to feel loved and supported as I change and grow.

Self-Talk

I monitor my self-talk.

When I hear criticism, "shoulds," and put
downs, I override them with positive,
encouraging, nonjudgmental words.

If I hear negative comments from others
directed to me, I will not let this stick in
my mind.

I will talk to them in person, if appropriate, or
have a conversation with them in my
mind as it is important to have the part of
me that feels shut down and unworthy
express my point of view.

I talk kindly to myself today.

Avoidance

Today, I pay attention to what makes me uncomfortable.

I notice the things I want to avoid. I pay attention to my body awareness and the feelings that come up for me.

I choose to stay with my discomfort knowing it is showing me something.

I then ponder the thoughts and feelings to determine what I need to do with the information, if anything.

Sometimes just being aware of what is taking place is enough.

I face what makes me
feel uncomfortable.

Expectations

Today, I accept where I am in my growth.
I can expect too much from myself
    sometimes.
It no longer serves me to expect myself to
    be farther along the path of life.
I can only be where I am.
I build my self-esteem by knowing where I
    am going and knowing it takes time to
    put into practice what I have learned.

*I let go of expecting too much, too fast
from myself.*

Strength

Today I ask the Higher Power for strength.
As I become more and more aware of the
   places that I need to take risks in order to
   grow in a healthy direction, I choose to fill
   myself from Spirit.
My Higher Self receives radiant light energy
   from Spirit and adjusts it to the perfect
   frequency for me.
I imagine a shower of golden energy
   flowing in, around, and through me from
   a point above my head.

*I am strong because I fill myself with
energy from Spirit.*

Spiritual Arrogance

Today, I pay attention and respond in an appropriate manner for my level of spiritual awareness rather than acting as if I were farther along my spiritual path than I really am.

Spiritual arrogance can trick me if I am not aware.

I realize where I am at this moment without putting myself down or pumping myself up.

Both are inappropriate for my growth.

I practice being realistic by accepting where I am in my spiritual growth.

Magical Day

Today is a special bonus day.
I allow my inner secret wishes, hopes, and
    dreams to be known to myself.
I write them down in my journal so that I
    remember what they are.
As I become aware of what I want, this
    awareness plants seeds in the garden of
    my mind; they then become potential
    goals.
What I feel I want combined with what I see
    in my mind moves me in that direction.

*My path appears as I allow my wishes,
hopes, and dreams to surface.*

Grounding

I work on grounding myself today.

I picture my feet planted firmly on the
ground.

I see Mother Earth radiating energy up
through the bottom of my feet,
energizing me.

I feel the solid feeling of being in my
physical body; I notice the boundary of
my skin.

As I remember to connect to this solid
place, I remain centered as I go through
life's experiences.

It helps me think clearly and take care of
myself.

I ground myself with the support of Mother Earth.

Improving

Each time I see what another person could
do to improve his or her life, I bring my
attention back to myself.

I am the only person I can change; I have
no control over others.

Each person can only act according to his
or her level of awareness.

I have enough to work on to improve
myself.

I work only on changing myself;
changing others is not my responsibility.

Teacher

Today, I remind myself that everyone is my
   teacher.
I choose to learn from the people I dislike as
   well as from those I like.
I pay attention to what my teachers are
   mirroring for me today.
I would not see something in another unless
   I also have it within me.
My power to express my goodness
   increases as I see what I like and dislike
   reflected by the teachers in my life.

*I see everyone as my teacher; they
reflect parts of myself.*

Blinders

Sometimes it is easy to wish I could go back to being less responsible for my life: that I could put up blinders and not see so much.

As I see parts of myself that I do not like, I continue to look.

In reality, I cannot put blinders up and go back to being unaware.

I can, however, choose to love and comfort myself.

I can take a break from the fast track of self-discovery.

A slower pace is nurturing sometimes.

*I slow the pace of self-discovery
when I get tired.*

One Day

I remind myself to live one day at a time.
When changes need to be made, it can be
    overwhelming.
It is appropriate to take risks and to set new
    goals, but thinking too much about the
    future robs me of my good feelings
    today.
I remember to live today and focus on only
    what is appropriate for my growth right
    now.

I live one day at a time.

Heart Opening

I ask for the courage to open my heart to
the love and support that is in my life.
I let it in.
Asking for help is a sign of strength and
humility.
I release the fears from the past that
impede my growth.
I trust the process of opening my heart to
experience love.

*I open my heart to receive
love and support.*

Inner Female

My female side knows how to love and
nurture myself and others.
I turn inward today to listen to and to feel
this wisdom.
Lessons in bonding with others are my
curriculum today.
I notice when I put up emotional
boundaries in relating to others.
I integrate the gentleness of my inner
female into the greater me.

*I follow the guidance of my inner
female today.*

Inner Male

My inner male knows how to protect and
    encourage me when I go out into the
    world.
I listen to the wisdom of this part of my
    consciousness today.
I notice situations when I do not take care
    of and protect myself.
When I need help or encouragement, I will
    draw on the strength of my inner male.

*I receive encouragement and protection
from my inner male.*

Journal

I write my thoughts, feelings, and insights in
    a journal.
I record my reactions to people and events,
    and I relate them to what my lessons for
    growth are during this passage of my life.
My pain, sadness, anger, hurts, and fears
    are eased as I write them down.
I receive clarity when I put what I feel into
    words.
I also write my feelings of joy,
    connectedness, comfort, and love.

*I keep a journal to help me grow and
integrate my inner feelings and reactions.*

Risks

I take a risk today that moves me out of a "stuck" pattern.

If I am unsure of what to do, I try something different.

Trial and error eventually will present something that works for me.

I hold something in my right hand, such as an acorn, to anchor me and remind me of my intention to break out of a "stuck" or crystallized pattern.

A small risk is just as important as a giant risk.

I take risks to break out of unwanted habits and patterns.

Visualization

I think about what I want.

I can create only from the possibilities of what I see in my mind.

As I focus on what I want by using my creative power of visualization, I put energy into creating.

I explore alternative realities with my mind in order to see which ones I really want.

I add power to these pictures by affirming and feeling the pictures as if they are a current reality.

I visualize what I want in order to make positive changes.

Information

I gather information today to make positive
　　changes in my life.
I read or listen to tapes that serve my
　　awareness.
Many teachers have put their ideas in
　　books and/or tapes that can help me.
I take in information with an open mind
　　using my thinking skills and body
　　awareness to decide what is wise
　　information for me to consider.
I notice if I feel good or bad after exposure
　　to new teachings.
I also notice if I feel less confused or more
　　confused.

*I listen to my Inner Self to determine
whether or not to follow a certain teacher.*

Time Alone

I spend at least half an hour today to think,
ponder, daydream, journal write,
meditate, or pray.
This time alone is a gift to myself to calm
and center myself so I can make the
changes in my life that I need to make.
I will spend this quality time with myself each
and every day.

*I spend time alone to think, to feel, and
to heal.*

Healthy People

I spend time with people who reflect my
inner beauty and love, people who are
growing and working on improving
themselves, and people who love
themselves.
This helps me to make positive changes.
Their skills rub off on me which helps when I
must work or live with unaware people.

*I spend time with healthy people who
reflect my wholeness.*

Hidden Meaning

I look for the meaning behind unwanted
   experiences.
This helps me grow.
I am like a detective investigating what part
   I play in these experiences so that I can
   stop repeating them.
When I see the "big picture," it helps me
   understand what is happening.
Then I can choose other behaviors, thinking
   patterns, or attitudes.

*I look for hidden meaning in my
experiences in order to grow
in consciousness.*

Courage

I have the courage to take another step
   towards fully loving myself.
I allow old feelings of devaluing myself to
   come to the surface.
After feeling them, I release them.
New feelings of lightness and aliveness flow
   into me.

*I ask for courage to release old feelings
of unworthiness and to fill myself with
feelings of warmth and tenderness.*

Confidence

I remember that from the acorn, a sapling
   has grown with its early branches barren
   and stunted.
It is time to grow those branches more fully.
One of them is confidence.
I am learning to feel confident as I gain
   comfort in being who I am on the inside.
I then take new risks to bring about
   balance and wholeness.

*I am growing confidence from within to
be exactly who I am.*

Trust

I trust the universe to support my growth into
my Full-Potential Self.

It matters not in what order I learn lessons to
be whole and complete .

At the end of my life, looking back, it will not
matter whether I trusted at birth or at
age forty or seventy-five.

It only matters that I learned to trust.

---

*I trust the process that I am unfolding
into my Full-Potential Self.*

Communion

I pay special attention to being connected
to nature.
Moments of being in the silence of beauty
enhances the blending of Spirit and
matter.
A moment in the sunlight or rain with the
breeze and plants, birds, and animals
stills my mind to feel the power behind
such beauty.

*I commune with nature
to still my mind.*

Pain

I listen to any pain I have inside of me
whether it be physical, emotional,
mental, or spiritual.
Pain easily talks to me and brings insight into
the light.
As I understand and make changes, my
pain leaves.
It has served its purpose which was to get
my attention.

*As I listen to my pain, I hear the
messages guiding me to change.*

Being Right

I let go of needing to prove I am right.
It separates me from others who do not
   take my position.
Instead, I accept the fact that others may
   disagree with me and sometimes may
   not even want to know why I think or feel
   a certain way.
As I become secure in myself, I do not insist
   on being right.

*My good feelings about myself are not
determined by others' understanding or
agreeing with me.*

Deserving

I deserve love.
I release early teachings that led me to
    believe I was unworthy of love until I
    earned it.
I feel the warmth and love of my Higher Self
    pour down upon me healing the pain
    caused by the old beliefs.

I deserve and accept love in my life.

Inner Strength

I have the inner strength to meet the
   challenging experiences drawn into
   my life.
I remember to love and honor myself and
   to fill myself with healing energy from
   both the earth and Spirit.
As I center myself and feel solid in my
   physical form, I meet my day prepared.

*My inner strength carries me easily
through my challenges of the day.*

Alone

I set aside a special time to be alone with
myself, away from the demands of the
world.
I enjoy being with myself.
If any feelings of fear of loneliness present
themselves to me, I remember I am
never separate from my Higher Self.
I feel this connection with my Source as I
experience the silence of being alone.

I enjoy being alone with myself.

Masks

I let go of the masks of who I think I should
  be.
These masks served me from an earlier part
  of my life; they were the only defenses I
  knew how to use in order to survive.
My protection comes from the awareness I
  now have.
I can still choose to wear a mask at times
  when I know no other options.
This is temporary, however, because I am
  learning day by day to be myself
  regardless of other people's reactions to
  me.

*I no longer need masks to hide my Inner
Self. I am enough all by myself.*

Power

I claim the power to be me.
I choose to express who I am on the inside.
I release comparing myself to other people.
I continue to discover the blueprint of my
    Full-Potential Self.
I release any parts of me acting through the
    mask of who I am not.
False expressions of me are no longer
    needed for my growth.
My inner beauty is ready to shine.

*I empower myself by being only
my True Self.*

Loving Kindness

I choose to live my life with loving kindness
even though I may appear to be soft
and vulnerable and easily hurt.
I, however, have a strength from within that
is able to set boundaries so others
cannot take advantage of me.
I choose these boundaries with awareness
and with an open heart that knows
loving kindness.
Sometimes the most kind and loving thing
to do is raise my voice or confront.
At other times, it is to remain silent and
remove myself from the drama.

*I choose to live my life with
loving kindness.*

Unhappiness

I feel unhappy when I am not honoring
   myself and have wandered off my life
   path.
As I learn to experience inner peace and
   live my life with awareness, I make
   choices that feel joyful.
I listen to the unhappy feelings so I can go
   within to find out what is needed for a
   correction.
Quiet time alone or with a special friend or
   spiritual teacher gives me the insight to
   make necessary changes.

*I listen to the messages my unhappy
feelings give me.*

Joy

Joy provides feedback that I am on track
and that I am living from my soul.

As I learn to connect with my soul, I learn
what my natural state is.

When I am in this place of soul connection, I
easily go through the process of
experiencing.

Even when things are difficult for my
personality self (the physical, emotional,
and mental sides of me), this soul
connection allows me to connect with
my Spiritual Self, and I can be joyful.

When I have spiritual awareness, I
understand why I experience certain
things.

As I grow in my spiritual awareness,
I allow joy to radiate from within.

Enjoyment

I pay attention to the things in life that give
me enjoyment.
Today, I choose to enjoy my day.
Even if something unexpected comes up
that throws me off center, I remember to
put things for enjoyment into my day.
One difficult moment does not ruin my
whole day.

I choose to enjoy my day.

The Journey

I allow my goals to guide me, and I remain
   conscious of the process.
The journey is the real goal.
As soon as I achieve one goal, there is
   always another and then another.
I find enjoyment in the journey.
Life is a process which I enter freely.
I accept the journey that is my life.

The journey of life is my ultimate goal.

Playfulness

I enter the day with the intention to play.
I look for ways to laugh as I celebrate April Fool's Day.
I really pay attention when a child or friend plays a joke on me. I let go of being serious; it is a day to be playful.
My inner child looks for simple ways to play and joke.

I let go and play.

Growth

I learn from everyone and everything that
   happens in my day.
As I make positive changes, I notice
   reactions both from within myself as well
   as from others.
I broaden my horizons when I pay attention
   to the times when I feel resistance from
   myself and others, as well as when I
   receive encouragement.
As I stay conscious, I receive insights into
   what maintains my growth and what
   stops my growth.

*Everything that comes my way is an
opportunity for my growth.*

Behavior

I am a spiritual being and am worthy even if
my behavior is bad.
I love and accept myself even when I do
not like my actions, habits, or
performance.
My self-esteem is no longer based on the
results of my behavior.
By separating my behavior from the spiritual
me, I know and feel my goodness.

I separate my behavior from the real me.

Growing

I am growing in many ways.
I notice the difference between my
    physical, emotional, mental, and spiritual
    needs.
I nurture the part of me that is in most need
    today.
The whole gestalt that I am benefits as this
    part of me is nurtured and is able to
    grow.

*I feed myself physically, emotionally,
mentally, and spiritually in order to
grow in a positive way.*

Perfect Order

At each stage in my growth and
   development, I am perfect being who I
   am.
I am doing only what I am capable of
   doing at each stage based on my
   awareness.
I honor the process of perfection unfolding
   in my consciousness.

*Each stage of my life unfolds in
perfect order.*

Life Challenges

Life challenges open my eyes to
  unconscious aspects of myself.
Without resistance and challenge, I would
  not notice or pay attention.
I grow as I experience a life challenge.
Though I may not sail through the passage
  of a life challenge, I remain aware in
  order to grow in consciousness.
I keep my spiritual eyes open to grow in
  conscious awareness of Self.

*I accept my life challenges as
opportunities for my growth and
awareness.*

Genuine Encounters

I am genuine in all my interactions with
others.
Only I can know for sure if I have a genuine
intention.
I am sincere and honest with myself and let
go of false pretenses.
I choose to relate from the heart of my true
Self.

*I am learning to be genuine in all my
relationships with others.*

Inner Vision

I do not judge anything I see today.
Instead, I look behind the circumstances of
my life for greater meaning and purpose.
I expand my inner vision to see what is really
going on.
I look for patterns that repeat themselves
rather than see myself as the effect of
these circumstances.
I see the patterns that are healthy and
those that are unhealthy and need
changing.

*My inner vision shows me what is
really going on behind circumstances.*

Evolution

I see my life evolving into greater meaning
and purpose.

Everything I think, feel, and do gives me
experiences to explore the meaning of
my life.

Today, I notice the unity of all life and feel
my place in it.

I spend time appreciating some aspect of
nature which connects me to this greater
unity.

I accept the process of evolution.
My life has purpose and meaning.

Self-Esteem

I am part of the greater universe.
My little self is part of my Greater Self.
I accept this connection and allow love
    from the Greater Self to nourish my little
    personality self which still gets caught up
    in the drama of life.
When I forget to love myself, I tune into this
    greater love coming from Self.

I receive love from my Greater Self.

Importance of My Life

My life is important and counts.
I do not receive more or less value than
    anyone else.
It is important that I be who and what I am.
My life matters, and I make a difference. I
    am alive and, therefore, have a reason
    for being.
I allow the purpose of my life to unfold.

My life is important.
I make a difference.

Perfection

Today, I look at the perfection of my life
which includes all the imperfections.
I am like that oak tree growing into greater
degrees of maturity, perfect at each
stage of growth.
I accept each stage of my growth and
development without judgment.

***I am perfect at each stage of
my development.***

Challenges

I acknowledge and respond to my life
    challenges as they occur.
Avoiding them or denying them keeps me
    unaware.
As I do not like the surprise of hidden
    challenges that pop up when I least
    expect them, I gather information and
    take the risks necessary to meet these
    challenges and transform them.
This keeps me from repeating them which
    causes me unnecessary pain.

*I accept responsibility for transforming
my life challenges.*

Knowing Self

I am the person I spend the most time with
so it is important to know myself inside
and out.
It is not selfish to spend time knowing who I
am, what my thoughts and beliefs are,
and what my feelings are.
When I know myself, I avoid being
manipulated by others or by life's
circumstances.
I prepare myself by knowing myself well.

*I spend time
getting to know myself.*

Openness

I practice being open with myself and
   others today.
I use my intuition to give me feedback on
   how open to be.
I notice when others can match my
   openness and when they cannot.
I avoid setting myself up to be victimized by
   staying conscious while I am open to
   others less open to me.
My protection is my awareness.

*Staying consciously aware, I am open
with myself and others.*

Listening and Talking

In communicating with others, I balance my
     listening with my talking.
If either is lacking, I miss a chance to learn
     and grow in my relationships.
Both listening and talking are necessary in
     healthy relating.
It is important to really listen, not just remain
     silent, when relating to others.
It is also important to talk so that others can
     begin to understand me.

*I balance my listening and talking
with others.*

Consequences as Teachers

I allow myself to say, think, and do whatever I choose without judging my value by the outcome.

All of my thoughts, words, and actions have consequences.

Some consequences will teach me to repeat beliefs, words, and behaviors while others will teach me that I do not choose to repeat them.

I pay attention to consequences. However, I no longer judge my value based on these consequences.

Patterns

I choose to see the patterns of my life.
Painful patterns from my early conditioning
    surface so that I can release feelings of
    powerlessness.
Once I see a pattern repeating, (the
    people may be different but the
    circumstances are similar), I then have
    the free will to do something differently.

My past patterns no longer control me.
I see them and make new choices.

Repressed Feelings

I allow feelings to surface as I am ready to process them.

Sometimes my freedom to enjoy the present is stopped by repressed feelings.

I surround myself with love, and I breathe deeply and ask myself to bring forward a situation from the past that is not resolved, understood, or even conscious.

I close my eyes and scan the years of my life.

As I choose a time period, I patiently choose one incident to work on.

As feelings come up, I may need to cry or hit a pillow.

I journal write and then go for a walk to feel the healing power of nature.

I seek outside help when I need additional support.

I allow repressed feelings to surface in order to transform them into the light of understanding and forgiveness.

Emotional Reactions

I notice the emotional outbursts and strong
    reactions I have today.
They are clues to the unconscious issues
    that I have to resolve.
When I am alone, I take the time to ask
    myself how the current person or situation
    is part of a greater pattern.
As I do this, I find it easier and easier to
    forgive the current situation and to have
    a healthy response based on current
    feelings and reactions.

*I am learning to respond with wisdom
rather than overreact to
people and events.*

Asking

I ask for what I need and want; then I let go
and allow the universe to respond.
If another person is involved, I receive what
they are capable of giving.
I am open to new or different ways of
getting my wants and needs met.
Sometimes I have to wait for proper timing
or until after I remove my blocks to
receiving.

*I let my needs and wants be known and
allow them to be met, sometimes, in
unexpected ways.*

Looking Beyond Duality

I accept that there is meaning in everything
    that happens to me.

I look behind judgments of good and bad
    to see what the hidden aspects are in
    situations that are difficult for me to
    accept.

I look for a third option whenever I am
    caught in an "either/or" situation.

*I look for meaningful choices of
thoughts, words, and actions that move
me beyond duality thinking of
"either/or."*

Excitement

I look for what ignites my interest in life.
This feeling gives me feedback on what is
stimulating to me.
I pay attention to my inner needs to
determine whether I need more or less
excitement in my day.
It is important to find some excitement in
each day to enjoy living.

*I am excited about my day. This
excitement gives joy to my life.*

The Psychic Buck

I pay attention to where I need to take
   responsibility for my life.
I no longer pass the psychic buck to
   someone else.
For example, I may have the power to have
   most of the world agreeing that I am a
   victim.
This may give me sympathy; however, it
   stops my growth and keeps me stuck in
   the victim pattern.
I no longer pass this responsibility on to
   another.

*I accept responsibility for my life. The
psychic buck stops here.*

Enmeshment

I disentangle myself from enmeshment in
    other people's boundaries.
I notice when I lose a sense of self and am
    caught up in other people's dramas.
I stop being the one to make everyone feel
    better at the expense of taking care of
    myself.

I am clear with my boundaries to
avoid enmeshment into
other people's problems
and emotional reactions.

Balance

I pay attention to my needs and wants
observing how they affect the people
around me.
I have the desire to balance my needs with
other people's needs.
When in conflict, I determine, to the best of
my ability, who has the greater need at
the time so that person (whether it's me
or not) can receive first.
I choose not to dominate or be dominated.
The balance of give and take is important in
my close relationships.

*I balance my needs with the
needs of others.*

Right Action

I tune into my Inner Self to determine what is
   right for me to do in each situation I
   experience in life.

When unclear, I go to a quiet place to think,
   then I am able to see beyond emotional
   and defensive reactions.

No one can tell me what I should do; they
   can only tell me what they might do in
   my situation.

I get clear with myself on what my motives
   are for any action; so that right action will
   follow.

I allow right action to flow through me.

Wise Use of Power

I pay attention today to how I use my
power.
I notice if I feel powerless or powerful.
I empower myself with kindness and love so
that I can use my power wisely.
If I dominate and force my will over another,
I notice this and make amends.
In learning to use my power wisely, I may
make mistakes and experience extremes
sometimes.
Staying conscious makes me able to make
corrections.

I use my power wisely.

Loving Kindness

I live my life from a position of love.

I am clear that coming from an intention of love does not dictate any specific behavior.

Sometimes the most loving thing to do is to remove myself from a situation or to confront another.

All I need do is focus on this intention to come from loving kindness and to practice it on myself as well as on others.

I live my life from the place of loving kindness.

Encouragement

I give myself encouragement to move
   forward on healing myself.
I talk gently, but firmly, to myself as I move
   forward on my journey.
I take the risks to change my unwanted
   patterns of thinking and behaving even
   though it may feel unfamiliar and
   uncomfortable.
I know I can change; I can keep going.

*I encourage myself to take another step
forward in healing myself, my
relationships, and the earth.*

Honoring Myself

I honor myself today.
I respect and appreciate the beauty and
    perfection of who I am.
I treat myself with the love and respect that
    I show to others.
It is a privilege to be who I am as I learn and
    grow in consciousness.

*I honor myself with the respect, love,
and reverence of a Sacred Being.*

Trusting Intuition

My only real protection in life is being able
   to trust my intuition.
As I learn to trust my intuition, I become
   aware that I am safe.
Situations and people are perceived by my
   five senses — sight, hearing, touch, taste,
   and smell.
These senses are not always enough to give
   me information to make wise choices.
My intuition gives me the missing
   information.
My intuition can help me discover life-
   purpose choices or more basic survival-
   level choices such as who to trust (by
   feeling and knowing when someone's
   intentions are incongruent with their
   actions) or when a dangerous situation is
   to be avoided.
My intuition allows me to stop depending
   on other people to take care of me.

*I listen to my inner guidance. My
intuition guides and protects me.*

Evaluating Self

I stop evaluating my worth by measuring myself against my expectations.

It is good to have standards and to be aware of my values.

Today I take stock of how I think I am doing in living my values and standards.

I may need to list my values to become more aware of them.

I eliminate any that say I should value something based on someone else's value system (unless I feel it is "right" for me).

I notice progress I have made; small steps are important.

If I have feelings of failure, I use them for motivation and begin again to meet my internal standards.

I evaluate myself today to see my progress. I feel good when I live by my values and standards.

Power to Choose

I have the power to choose my thoughts
and behavior.
I can improve how I feel by either changing
my thoughts or my behavior.
I choose one thought or one behavior to
work on today.
I will see myself improving this thought or
behavior.
Every time I begin to think or act in the old
way, I will gently refocus on the new idea
I'm learning.

*I have the power to feel better by
choosing better thoughts or behaviors.
I visualize the new thought or behavior
over and over to help me live it.*

Body Awareness

I focus on relaxing my body today.

I take deep breaths to use more of my lung capacity which calms me and lessens my stress level.

I pull myself up by an imaginary string at the top of my head which is connected to the top of my spine.

I allow my arms to hang loose.

I balance on my feet and allow the ankle bone, knee, hip, shoulder, and ear to align.

I move my arms and torso when I walk.

I live comfortably in my body. By deep breathing and aligning my skeletal system, I receive the support I need.

Focus

I pay attention to where I am going.
I focus on what I want to accomplish today.
I begin by performing simple tasks such as
making my bed or making a phone call.
I step towards meeting a hidden desire.
When I focus on what I want, I know which
direction to take even when all the steps
are not clear.

*I focus on what I want so I can move in
that direction.*

Emotional Strength

I am emotionally strong.
I know that no matter what other people
   say or do to me, they cannot take away
   my awareness that I am a worthwhile
   person.
My inner life is mine and nothing can take
   away my realization of my innate worth.

I am a worthwhile person no matter
what others say or do to me.

Daily Goals

I like to know what I will do with my day.
I write a list of goals I wish to accomplish
  each morning.
My list of goals includes time to think and
  work on myself.
I respond to my physical and emotional
  cycles.
Sometimes I move quicker than at other
  times.
It nurtures me to manage my time.

I set daily goals to use my time wisely.

Making a Difference

My life counts in the grand scheme of
    things.
I make a difference.
I am to be me, and no one else can take
    my place.
I allow my inner feelings to guide me on
    where I can use my talents to make a
    better world.
I begin with thinking good thoughts about
    myself, and I pursue possibilities of getting
    involved where I can contribute.

I make a difference; my life counts.

My Body

I take care of my body.
Connecting spiritually, attuning to my
   intuition, and connecting with my Higher
   Self are easier when my body is running
   smoothly.
I work from where my body is presently, not
   comparing myself to other people or to
   me in the past.
I eat foods that promote my good health.
I exercise and get proper rest.

*My body is my friend, and I
take care of it.*

Helping Others

I like to help others.

I get my own needs met so that I have energy to give to others.

Service performed from my overflow of energy balances me.

I pay attention to what others' needs are, which may be different from making things "nice" for them or doing what they may need to be doing for themselves.

I like to help others. I serve from a place of balancing my needs with others' needs.

Love

I remember who I am. I am Love.
I am a worthy part of the Universe.
I am okay, and I deserve to take care of
    myself, get my needs met, and create
    what I want.
This simple message is the most important
    step in my journey.

I am Love.

Authority of My Soul

Eventually, I have to listen to my soul and comply with what the spiritual agenda is for me.

This takes courage, a willingness to break out of old patterns, and a willingness to keep growing in order to heal my early conditioning.

When I listen, my life really gets easier.

I find my way through the rough passages and share the wisdom I have gained with others.

I listen to the authority of my soul.

Curiosity

I am curious about everything around me.
I learn more and more about myself when I
    pay attention and question people,
    events, feelings, thoughts, reactions, etc.
    in my environment.
It is good to use my curiosity; it takes me into
    realms of greater understanding.

I learn about myself by being curious
about everything in my environment.

Open-Mindedness

I open my mind to new ideas outside of my
present belief system.

Rather than disagree or put down a new
idea, I consider the possibility of its truth.

I gather more information about the idea
before deciding whether or not it is of
value to me.

I observe people who believe this new way
in order to determine if they are
expressing incongruities or if they have
an inner peace about them.

*I have a free and open mind to explore
new ideas.*

Contribution

As I feel better and better about myself, I have the ability to contribute to those around me and to the greater service of humanity.

I want to give back what I receive in order to keep the cycle of giving and receiving flowing.

I automatically give by being in a positive state of mind as I grow into greater and greater awareness.

It is just as important to give a smile and to reply kindly to the grocery checker as it is to join the Peace Corps or to run my business with the bottom line of human kindness; all make a contribution to the healing of the world.

I make a contribution to the world by first learning to feel good about myself and then passing human kindness on to others.

Shame

I release my feelings of shame.
I detach myself from being embarrassed
    about having needs.
Everyone has needs.
My inner child has needs, and I am here to
    comfort and support my inner child.
The adults who raised me or taught me
    could only pass on to me reflections of
    their level of consciousness.
Today, I recognize their lack of awareness in
    the shame that was passed on to me.
I am good, and it is okay to have needs
    and to be needy at times.
I no longer have to be ashamed of these
    needs.

*I release feelings of shame; no one is to
blame. I am free to feel my feelings,
even the needy dependent ones.*

Motivation

I am motivated to improve my life.
I first see in my mind's eye the probabilities
   that will benefit me.
Once I can see a future action that excites
   me and benefits me, I am automatically
   motivated.
The more I go within to determine what is
   right for me, the more my inner urges and
   pictures emerge to guide and motivate
   me.

*Once I see the way to go, I easily
motivate myself.*

Real Needs

I go within to get in touch with my real
    needs.
I may have been conditioned by outer
    needs for success, popularity, and
    achievement coming from parents,
    teachers, peers, T.V., etc.
I may have missed a whole set of inner
    needs: ones that come from within me.
These are my real needs.
Wise motivation comes from getting to
    these real needs.

*I go within to discover my real needs as
they provide the motivation to create
my life in the perfect way for me.*

My Shadow

I pay attention to traits in others that I do
not like.

Whatever I disown in myself shows up in
other people.

By owning my shadow or dark side (those
parts of myself that I do not like and have
made unconscious to myself), I take
responsibility for my life.

I am capable of all actions, thoughts, and
feelings, good as well as evil.

Rather than judge or be victimized by
people with certain traits, I acknowledge
that they are hidden parts of me.

I get to choose what to act on from my
shadow side when it is made conscious.

I lose my power of choice when I project it
onto another person and call them bad
or evil.

---

*I allow my shadow to come into my
awareness at the pace I can handle. I
empower myself by owning
this side of me.*

Well-Being

I allow myself to feel good.

I get a sense of well-being by accepting that I am good and doing the best that I can at each moment with my level of awareness.

I no longer compare myself to anyone.

I am growing in consciousness at the perfect pace for me.

I accept inner peace by choosing to feel good and by having a strong, positive sense of well-being.

My sense of well-being gives me inner peace and strength to go forward.

Weighing Consequences

I make choices today by looking at the
 probable outcomes.
I weigh the consequences of each choice
 to determine the wisest choice for me.
If I am willing to pay the consequences,
 then I am free to make any choice.
I take responsibility for my choices, both
 wise and unwise.

*I make wise choices by weighing
consequences before I choose.*

Free Will

I look at my free will to make choices.

If I am aware of my true needs, then I can
use my free will to make choices that
support my highest good and my
understanding of myself.

If I am on the fence between two choices, I
work on expanding my awareness of my
Inner Self.

The awareness of my inner needs helps me
take the risks involved in exercising my
free will.

Others will make choices for me if I do not.

Not making a choice also is a choice.

*I accept the privilege of having free
will. I use my free will to make
conscious choices.*

Gentle Strength

I use my gentle strength to move forward today.

I take note of situations when I need to confront and make a change.

I overcome the fear of using my power to get what I want or need.

If I feel overpowered by something or someone, I may need to use my power to get results.

I use my gentle side at the same time in order not to overcorrect.

(Sometimes I go from one extreme of feeling powerless and victimized to the other extreme of feeling powerful and victimizing).

The in-between place of knowing my limits, boundaries, and desires and, at the same time, being flexible and responsive are called forth with gentle strength.

I use my gentle strength when I need to confront and make a change.

Inner Freedom

I am free because I am growing and
    getting to know myself.
I understand why I do many things which
    gives me the power of using my free will
    to improve my life and solve my
    problems.
My inner freedom allows me to watch
    myself in my interactions with others and
    to disengage from the drama.
When I see how and why I got to this
    moment, I have incredible inner
    freedom.

I am free because I have inner freedom.

Humility

I acknowledge myself for who and what
and why I am.
This gives me the opportunity to live my life
with humility.
I no longer have the need to have every
good deed or accomplishment
acknowledged by others.
I take private joy in living my life with quiet
humility.

*I am humble because I no longer have
the need to prove myself.*

Value-Judging

I stop value-judging others and let them live
by their own code of values.

I am secure in my values.

I have no need to impose my values on
others who do not agree with me.

I allow others to have their value system
without judgment from me.

I notice when I make others wrong in my
mind.

This gives me the opportunity to fine tune
my release of value-judging.

I choose to live my life free of validating
myself based on whether or not other
people agree with me.

---

*I am secure in my value system and no
longer need agreement from others to
feel good.*

Physical Health

I take care of my physical self.
No matter how good my intentions are to
    take risks or to emotionally feel good, I
    can only do so to the degree that my
    physical body is balanced and well.
I take care of any imbalances in diet,
    exercise, or sleep.
I get help from professionals if necessary.

I improve my physical health. My
strong physical mechanism allows
more Spirit to operate through me.

Strengths

I list my strengths and the things I can do.
I need to remind myself often of my full
potential for goodness and higher
consciousness.
When I express myself from this set of
strengths, I meet my challenges better.
I then motivate myself to express my talents,
connect to others, and feel good about
myself.

*I see and appreciate my strengths. I am
proud of the things I can do.*

Memorial Day

I pay tribute to others who died in wars.
I forgive the consciousness in those times for using physical violence to settle power struggles which was the only way humanity at that time knew how to settle conflicts with other countries.
I am grateful to be alive today when this consciousness is in the process of changing.
I do my part to eliminate the power of war to exist on the planet by solving my personal power struggles through communication, love, and empowering my opponents.
When each of us feels safe, loved, and powerful, the world will no longer need to use physical force or authoritarianism to settle disputes.

I solve my power struggles in nonviolent ways.

Survival

I am okay, and I know I am capable of surviving.

I have up to this point.

I am able to find my way when I stray from my path.

I can find answers within, as well as outside, myself.

I have the power now to attract people, information, and experiences that help me face my shadow or unconscious parts of myself.

When I illuminate with understanding what scares me, I find only light.

I am a survivor and able to transform my unconscious into conscious awareness.

Recovery

I am recovering from the illusions of my
    conditioned past and early childhood.
I am strong now that I have the tools to
    speed my recovery.
Energy that was blocked because of living
    from the illusion of fear, pain, and
    separation from my Spiritual Self is now
    available.
I am learning to create my life from this
    place of wholeness.

*I rejoice in the process of recovery that
has helped me awaken.*

New Ideas

I plant new ideas or seed thoughts in my
  mind.
I focus on inspirational ideas that suggest
  the direction of healing and wholeness
  for me.
A simple test to let me know this positive
  direction is to ask myself whether a
  certain teaching makes me feel good,
  connected to my Self, or whether it
  makes me feel fearful, shameful, and
  disconnected from my Self.
When I was one, two, and three years old, I
  trusted this ability to guide me.
I return to this inner guidance system so I
  can plant healthy seed thoughts in my
  consciousness.

*I plant new ideas in my mind that
inspire me to grow and change in the
direction of my highest good.*

Nourishment

I fertilize and water new seed thoughts in
    my mind so they will grow and serve me
    to live my life from my Full-Potential Self.
I repeat these seed thoughts over and over
    until they become a part of my new
    belief system.
I reinforce these new ideas by reading,
    taking classes, and being around other
    people who support and reflect these
    ideas.

*I give myself nourishment to help new
seed thoughts grow and blossom.*

Integration

I listen to the inner parts of myself.
Those parts that have conflict and pain
 need to learn blending and integration
 into the greater whole of me.
I listen to competing and immature aspects
 of myself so they will feel understood.
I love these parts of myself so they will feel
 safe to mature and will want to
 cooperate on the same team.
I need to integrate all aspects of myself to
 feel whole.
All parts of me have a positive intention
 somewhere.
Once I learn their positive intention, I can
 appreciate and call forth this energy as
 needed on the conscious level.

*I allow all parts of me to be heard so I
can blend and integrate their energy
into the service of my Higher Self.*

Organization

I organize my life on all levels.
I begin with the mundane by cleaning out
    my closets, drawers, files, and the trunk of
    my car.
I release items that no longer serve me.
If I do not use or like clothing or possessions,
    I give them away.
I next look at how I use my time.
I give myself permission to eliminate
    spending time doing things that do not
    support my growth or highest good.
I balance my time between doing and
    being.

I organize my possessions and time.

Life-Style Changes

I take a mental inventory today, noticing areas of my life in which I need a permanent change of habit.

I make a list of the new behaviors desired and I use them as goals.

A life-style change is a process that takes time and energy.

I give myself this needed time and forgive myself when I am not able to maintain new behaviors.

I read this list of goals often to impact my subconscious mind.

The more I feel a strong desire for this life-style change, the faster I create it.

I desire permanent life-style changes that support my new level of awareness.

Resistance

I notice when I resist people, ideas, suggestions, or inner wisdom.

I slow down and listen to my fears as they need to be expressed.

I honor my resistances as they show me where I need to spend time looking at unconscious blocks.

I can only progress as fast as my resistances will allow.

I learn from what I resist.

Spiritual Guidance

I ask for spiritual guidance to help me over
the rough spots.
The answers may come from direct
experience with the Source, in a book,
from T.V., or from another person.
I am receptive to help when it answers my
call for guidance.

*I receive help whenever I ask for
spiritual guidance.*

Humor

I allow myself to see humor in my life.
When I take myself too seriously, I miss
enjoying the moment by being "in my
head," practicing being right.
As I lighten up, I use laughter to make it
through many of the rough spots.
I notice feelings are expressed and tension
released when I laugh at myself.

I stop taking myself so seriously.
I laugh at myself.

Opening Communication

I open communication with those people I
care about.

I openly express myself and talk about my
feelings and experiences.

I let go of expectations of the other person.

I listen and do not offer suggestions unless
asked.

I listen "between the lines" to get the real
message the other person is sending and
respond to this rather than the exact
words.

I pay attention to nonverbal
communication such as body language
and tone of voice.

*I feel connected to loved ones when I
use open communication skills.*

Inner Resistance

I pay attention to my inner resistances to
others.
This tension may be felt in my body even if
my mind is able to rationalize and justify
my position or point of view.
As I release this inner resistance, I heal my
outer relationships with people.
Sometimes the healing of the relationship
requires that I remove myself from the
relationship, at least for a time, if it seems
that the situation will not change.

*I let go of my inner resistance to
other people.*

Courage

I have the courage to take another step towards fully loving myself.

As old feelings of devaluing myself arise, I allow them to surface.

I feel them and then let them go, cleansing my emotional body.

I imagine lying on the shore line at the edge of the beach, allowing the waves to wash over me.

As I feel the water subside, I imagine the old feelings dissolving into the ocean.

I stand up with courage to face my future empty and waiting for the new to blossom from within me.

I have the courage to move forward after emotionally cleansing my consciousness.

Confidence

I am confident and comfortable in being
 who I am.
As I trust in the perfection of who I am, I
 more easily take risks to grow into my
 wholeness.
I am perfect at each stage of my growth.

**I deserve to feel confident and self-
assured as I grow into my True Self.**

Trust

I trust the universe to bring me the perfect
   experience to support my growth into my
   Full-Potential Self.
I trust myself to perceive what is going on in
   relating with people and events.
Rather than trusting others to support me, I
   take responsibility to listen to my intuition.

*I trust my feelings, perceptions, and
intuition to take care of me.*

Communion

I connect to the outdoors today.
I choose one thing to relate to, such as a
tree, or a squirrel or a leaf or a cloud.
I allow a part of myself to exchange energy
with this magnificent part of nature.

*I enjoy communion with the Spirit
in nature .*

Body Pain

I listen to my pain so that I receive the
communication my body is sending.
I pay attention to where the pain is
registering in my body.
The body sends messages, even if I am
unaware of hurting emotions and
conflicting beliefs.
When I pay attention, I use the pain as
information that something is "off," and I
go within to discover the problem.
I thank my body for being such a sensitive
instrument registering conflict and calling
attention to changes I need to make.

*I am in rapport with my body. I listen
to my feelings to receive my
body's messages.*

Weeding the Garden

I take inventory today of all the things in my
life that I no longer want in the garden of
my life.

Seeds that were planted in less aware days
that are not in alignment with my present
consciousness need to be removed or
transplanted to where they are needed.

I look at my current surroundings and give
away what is no longer needed.

I do the same with guiding beliefs,
outmoded ideas, and thoughts that stop
my growth.

*I weed the garden of my life so new
seed thoughts can grow.*

Cause and Effect

I pay attention to the law of cause and
effect operating in my life.
I take note of what I like that is being
experienced.
I look behind this effect to see how I
created what is now happening.
As I expand this ability to see, I can repeat
what I like.
More and more, I am able to cause my life
to be the way I want it to be.

*I am empowered to be the cause in my
life. I remember always to tune into my
Higher Self.*

Playing My Hand

I play the hand I am dealt each day to the best of my ability.

Though some things appear to be challenging my ability to change, I expand my awareness in order to participate in the game of life.

I watch myself as I go through the challenging experiences.

Being the observer allows me to see that I can make changes.

I am good at playing the hand I am dealt each day.

My Best

My self-worth is not dependent on how well
   I live each day.
I am worthy because I am part of the
   Greater Whole living in physical
   expression.
I do the best I can to figure out the game
   called life.
As I live each day, I give it my best and pick
   myself up if I stumble.

*I keep going; I am doing my best
each day.*

Summer Solstice

I align myself to the greater order and
    rhythm of the earth.
I feel this year's day of greatest light.
Today, I read and ponder the significance
    of the Great Invocation written by Alice
    Bailey in 1936. (See the next page.)

*I align myself with the Greater Rhythm
of life's cycles.*

The Great Invocation

From the point of Light within the Mind of God
      Let light stream forth into the minds
      of men.
      Let Light descend on Earth.

From the point of Love within the Heart of God
      Let love stream forth into the
      hearts of men.
      May Christ return to Earth.

From the centre where the Will of God is known
      Let purpose guide the little wills of men -
      The purpose which the Masters
      know and serve.

From the centre which we call the race of men
      Let the Plan of Love and Light work out
      And may it seal the door where
      evil dwells.

Let Light and Love and Power restore the
  Plan on Earth.

This Invocation or Prayer does not belong to any person or group, but to all Humanity. The beauty and the strength of this Invocation lies in its simplicity, and in its expression of certain central truths which all men, innately and normally, accept - the truth of the existence of a basic Intelligence to Whom we vaguely give the name of God; the truth that behind all outer seeming, the motivating power of the universe is Love; the truth that a great Individuality came to earth, called by Christians, the Christ, and embodied that love so that we could understand; the truth that both love and intelligence are effects of what is called the Will of God; and finally the self-evident truth that only through *humanity* itself can the Divine Plan work out.

Alice A. Bailey,
in her book *From Bethlehem to Calvary*

Joy

I take joy in this moment and in this day.
I sometimes hurt in the process of being
    who I am and disengaging from what is
    dysfunctional.
I remain joyful from the level of my soul
    knowing that I have found the way.
I can change my conditioned past so that I
    am a whole, fully-functioning adult.

I am joyful because I have found my
way home to wholeness.

Conflicts

I spend time alone to process my conflicts
with other people.

I no longer suppress or deny my feelings as
they come up during or after a
confrontation.

I look behind the conflict to see what my
part is.

I ask myself questions such as, "What would
I do differently?", "What did I not see that
caught me off guard?", "What patterns
am I working on?", etc.

If I feel it would be beneficial, I talk it over
later with the other person.

*I process my thoughts and feelings after
experiencing conflict with another.*

Inner Child

I nurture my inner child today.
I pay attention to hidden dependency
    needs that I project onto others.
When I catch myself feeling low because
    another cannot hold or touch or listen, I
    remember to nurture my inner child.
I may close my eyes and picture myself at
    an early age and bring this part of me
    that needs nurturing to sit on the lap of
    my present self.
As I hold this child and love this child,
    she/he talks to me, and I listen.
I express my love and show the way to
    wholeness, sharing all that I have learned
    so the pain does not have to be
    reexperienced.

I spend time nurturing my inner child
whenever I feel
others have let me down.

Inner Work

I spend time doing inner work on myself so that I can steer my life out of pain and confusion.

I listen to my feelings and thoughts today in order to take my inner temperature.

This lets me know what I need to do today to fill myself.

If I need to be touched and no one else is available, I may schedule a massage or spend time with animals.

If I need to move my body, I may walk or exercise.

If I need stimulation for my mind, I may buy a new book or take a class or go to a lecture to feed my intellectual hunger.

If I feel disconnected from people, I may find a support group to join or a workshop to take or go to counseling.

I spend time doing the inner work necessary to solve my problems and fill myself.

Religious Guilt

I release guilt that is a result of breaking the
rules of religious dogma.

I now have permission to question, explore,
and decide how I wish to connect with
the Source.

Though I respect religious traditions, I look at
the symbolism behind the rituals and
ceremonies.

I allow the Higher Love, Will, and Power to
come into my life in ways that agree with
my particular personality.

It is no longer important how I worship the
Higher Power; it is only important that I
do.

I am loved, honored, and respected by
the Source of all creation
and I return this.

History

My history does not need to predict the future.

As I learn who I am, what my needs are, and how to expand my awareness, I look at the matrix of patterns that were formed in my family of origin.

As I notice the negative patterns, I look at how they were acted out or how I overcorrected and acted out the opposite.

I know that my power to move beyond the crystallization of these past negative patterns is in the moment.

I do not need to repeat these patterns because I am willing to look at my history and to remember it.

I am aware of my history so I can correct, in the present, any negativity I do not choose to take with me into the future.

Active Intelligence

I use my mind before I take action.
To break out of unneeded patterns, I must
    think before I act or speak.
My mind, used at its best, steers my
    consciousness to greater freedom,
    awareness, and wholeness.
I spend time thinking about what I need to
    do to grow into greater wholeness.
My intellect is my friend, and I think before
    taking action.

*I use active intelligence to bridge
between what I need to do and what I
am doing.*

Comfort

I seek nurturing and comfort when I find it
   necessary to change the pattern of
   acting out early negative patterns.
I do the work of self-healing by relying on
   my support systems.
I gladly accept the guidance of a teacher,
   mentor, or counselor to help me on this
   new path.
Without the maps and the wayshowers, I
   would randomly stumble along.
I receive comfort from those who show me
   the way.
I see that they can do it, and I know that I
   can also.

*I feel great comfort because I have
found people to show me the way.*

Dislikes

I learn from my dislikes.
What I do not like is the only internal
feedback I have sometimes.
I use this information to help me discover
what I do like and value.
I stop using my dislikes to complain or stay
stuck or to criticize either myself or others.
I pay attention to what makes me
uncomfortable, brings up criticism, or
plays "poor me" self-talk.
I ponder to discover what my dislikes are
really telling me about what I want to
create and experience and enjoy.

*I pay attention to and learn from what
I do not like. My dislikes give me clues
to what I really want.*

Depression

I listen to my inner needs when my emotions feel heavy, low, and out of sorts.

I spend quality time with myself when I am "down" emotionally.

I remember what anchors me and helps me get in touch with why I am feeling depressed.

I may receive nurturing from music, flowers, being in nature, being with animals or a pet, a cherished item from childhood, or a crystal, to name just a few.

As I tune into my Inner Self, I determine what needs attention.

I seek help from others if I cannot do this alone.

I listen to the feedback my Inner Self is giving me when I feel depressed.

Maintenance

I take care of my physical body and my
    material possessions.
I notice what needs to be fixed in my home
    (this means the physical space I live in).
I make a plan to take care of what is
    needing repair.
I may need a physical examination, to
    recover a chair, or to throw out
    unneeded items and clothing.
I spend the day paying attention to
    maintaining my physical world.

*I maintain my physical body
and possessions.*

Roadblocks

I make a list of the roadblocks in my
    consciousness that need leveling.
When I get in my own way, I stop my growth
    and awareness process.
By seeing the blocks, I know that my
    immediate agenda is to heal myself.
I create affirmations to move past these
    roadblocks.
For example, if I neglect spending time on
    my self growth, I may want to often say
    things such as, "I am worth an investment
    of time and energy," or "I choose to
    spend time learning why I do not like to
    take care of myself," or "I commit to
    reading five pages a day from a book
    that has information to help me solve my
    problems."

I face the roadblocks to my progress.
I create affirmations to know and
help myself.

The Land of Opportunity

I celebrate this land of opportunity.
I am grateful to live in a land with the theme
of personal freedom and opportunity
because I am free to live my life the way
I choose.
I meet this responsibility by becoming the
best I can be.
I choose to live up to this responsibility by
monitoring my actions, thoughts, and
feelings.
I wish this land of opportunity to continue in
freedom and peace for all its people.

I am grateful to live in this country,
which supports me growing into my
Full-Potential Self.

A Lighted House

I create a home and body that is full of light.

When I am infused with the Light of Spirit, I can light the way for others who are a step behind me on the path.

I allow the light to shine in all the dark corners of my physical home and physical body.

I release what is old and not needed as they collect dust in my closets and my consciousness.

I build a life in a lighted house: a place of refuge and comfort for myself and others.

Soul-Infused Personality

I watch as the dominance of my personality
wanes and the authority of my soul
waxes.

I am in the process of becoming a soul-
infused personality living from the place
of spiritual goodwill.

I need the personality as long as I am living
in a body in order to blend it with the
energy of my soul.

*I am a personality that is spiritually
motivated by the will of my soul.*

Path

The labyrinth was a diversion.
I leave behind the running around, as I now
know that I was lost and afraid to admit it.
I am no longer confused looking for, but not
finding, the exit.
The goal is my own healing which will allow
me to unify with the greater whole.
I am back on the path, and it feels good to
be home.
I am in the process of awakening to all I am
meant to be.

I am joyful to be on the path.

Secret

Wholeness is my secret.
I do not expect anyone to understand or
notice my journey into wholeness and
the integration of my many parts.
I release the need for those who are close
to me to understand where I am in
consciousness.
If I still need to share, I do so only with those
who are consciously working on
themselves.
I do not burden others who are not yet on
the path of awareness by sharing too
much of my spiritual journey.

My journey into wholeness is my secret.
It is not necessary for me
to have others notice.

Negative Thoughts

I pay attention to the thoughts I have about myself today.

I listen to the voice in my mind, paying strict attention to the negative thoughts.

I talk back to the negative self-talk telling it the new truths I am learning about my innate worthiness.

I ask people close to me, especially people in my family, what they believe are my negative thoughts about myself.

Usually the critical, negative, or judgmental things I say to others when I am upset gives me clues to what I am really saying to myself.

Once I discover this negative mind talk, I turn it around into positive, healthy affirmations and guiding beliefs.

I say kind, loving, and nurturing things to myself.

Loving Relationships

I have loving relationships to the degree
that I have a loving relationship with
myself.

Today, I begin improving my relationships by
working on myself.

I communicate my needs and wants and
listen to the people I love and care
about.

I practice unconditional acceptance of
myself and the people in my life.

I send warm and loving thoughts to my
partner, children, parents, siblings, friends,
neighbors, and co-workers.

I take the time to work on improving
relationships with those with whom I am
in conflict.

*I feel warm and loving towards all the
people in my life.*

Staying Present

I stay present in today's experiences.
I concern myself only with what I need to
    do today.
If I can do something today to effect
    tomorrow, then I do it.
Otherwise, I stop worrying about tomorrow.
If I redo and relive the past, I stop and
    remind myself to live in the present, the
    here and now.
I release myself from focusing on the past
    by remembering I need to forgive—-
    again and again if necessary.

I concern myself with the present.
This is enough to keep me busy.

Power

I am powerful because I am part of the
   creative Godforce and accept the
   assignment of creating my life.
I do this with joy and understanding. I am in
   charge of creating what I do with my life.
It feels good to be a powerful creator.

I am powerful.

Tolerance

I practice being tolerant today.
When people do not behave to my liking, I
    will be tolerant of them.
I will look behind their behavior to see why
    they do and say the things they do, then
    I will think through how I want to handle
    the situation.
I will change my reactions by being
    tolerant.
If I am being harmed and/or violated, I will
    remove myself from the situation.

I am tolerant of others today.

Limitations

I look at the boundaries of what I see as
    limitations in my life.
I explore to see if they are still valid.
I release outdated restrictions.
I look to the doorway to find a way out of
    my current limitations.
I walk through this threshold and enter a
    universe of unlimited potential.
I seek greater expansion.

*I release my limitations and walk
through the doorway of unlimited
potential. I am ready to expand
my horizons.*

Success

I accept every experience as part of the success of living my life.

If I have experiences that do not support my growth, I remember that they teach me choices that I do not want to make again.

Every day, I do better and better at living my life with a feeling of success.

I made it this far, and I have learned that being willing to take risks provides me with greater and greater successes.

I know my life is a success.

Shame

I give up being ashamed.
I let go of any thoughts, feelings, or actions
    that I feel are a mistake.
I no longer give fuel to this old feeling I
    learned in early life.
If I make a mistake, I am not bad.
If I have emotional dependency needs, I
    acknowledge them and do not hide
    from these needs.
I can only heal what I am aware of.
I fill my inner child that feels devalued with
    love and golden light.
I allow my grown-up self to nurture this inner
    child.

*I am proud to be me. I heal the parts of
me that do not feel whole and complete.*

Learning

I make a list of things I want to learn to do.
It does not matter how old I am or what my
physical limitations are.
If I am interested in developing a skill or
experiencing something, I put it on
the list.
I begin planning and daydreaming about
where to start.
I will read this list of things I want to learn
whenever I am bored.
This could be a perfect time to learn new
things.

Today I begin learning one new thing.

Roles

I make a list in my journal of all the roles I
    play.
I evaluate how these roles are supporting
    me.
Do I need to change some or renegotiate
    others?
I go within today to plan how to eliminate
    the roles that no longer serve me.
If I negatively affect people close to me, I
    begin talking to them about my
    awareness of my roles and what I might
    want to change.

I play my roles consciously.

Synchronicity

I look back at the series of coincidences
that have shaped my life.
I see the synchronicity (one or more events
which seem to be chance at first notice,
but in fact, are of great significance).
These events brought me to today even
though they went unnoticed at the time
they occurred.
I allow the universe to continue subtly
directing my life with synchronicity.

**I allow the wisdom of the universe to
direct my life. I notice the synchronicity
of events as I live my day.**

Angel

I feel the presence of my guardian angel
watching over me, guiding and
supporting me.
I allow this healing spiritual presence to boost
my power to love and protect myself.
I feel safe and secure.
I am open and receptive to insights to help
me understand my challenges from a
spiritual perspective.
I welcome my angel into my waking
consciousness.

*I accept the love and support and power
of my guardian angel.*

Flying

I am up here having made the jump,
proving that my spirit can fly.
As I look back, I see how this was the only
path I could take.
To the right and left and above and below,
I find new companions; they have been
waiting for me to ascend.
In front of me are those ready to guide and
show me the way.

I feel joy from taking the risk to fly
with Spirit. I am doing it now!

Ahead on the Path

Ahead of me I see light and openness
which is full of unrealized potential, the
material to create my future.
The raw materials are here in abundance.
I have earned this freedom of creation by
jumping off with my angel wings into this
uncharted territory in consciousness.

Ahead of me on the path, I see the light
of creative substance that is available
to me. I move toward greater and
greater potential.

Time

I have the time to do the things I want to
do.
If I am pressured with too many things to do,
I have a serious talk with myself today to
determine what needs to be released.
If I am bored and spend too much time
alone being passive, I also have a serious
talk with myself about being willing to
take risks and adding activity in my life.
I balance my time wisely between doing
and being.

*I use my time wisely so I have time to
do the things I want to do.*

Remembering

I remember who I am.
I am a spiritual being living in the school
    called Earth.
I am part of the Source of all things.
When I experience pain, fear, or anxiety, I
    soothe my little self by remembering who
    I really am.
My higher consciousness takes over when I
    remember, and I calm down and relax
    into knowing who I am.

*I remember that I am an important
part of the Universe.*

Light on the Path

The Light of Spirit illuminates my path.

I do not have to see the whole picture as I trust the Light to guide me to the next step.

As I turn around to review my life, I see the plan clearly and realize that it is a better plan than my personality self could have created.

I take each step trusting my Higher Self to guide me in the appropriate destination.

The light is on my path showing me the next step to take. I take this step with trust and anticipation.

I Am

I am a part of the universe and that makes
my life important.
The individual piece of consciousness that I
am is transformed daily as I expand my
awareness of myself and of life.
Each day I am a greater expression of my
Self.
I am the Source expressing in a physical,
emotional, mental, and spiritual unit
called ME.

*I am a conscious piece of the Universe,
growing and expressing as me.*

Children

I notice children today.
They help me remember the full potential in
  myself.
If I have my own children, I feel
  appreciation for them.
I remember the privilege it is to be their
  parent.
I express the love and gratitude I feel to my
  children.

*I love the children in my life. I express
my gratitude to them today.*

Living Love

I take one day at a time and live it to the
fullest.
This is living my purpose.
Even if I understand the greater significance
of my life, I can only live today's purpose.
Today, I tune into why I am really here: to
extend love, to be loved.

**I am one who leads the way in
living love.**

Present Moment

I no longer believe in coincidences in my
   life.
Everything that I have experienced has
   been important to bring me to this point
   in time.
I continue to put together the puzzle of who
   I am, so I can make sense of my life and
   see the purpose and plan behind outer
   appearances.

*Everything I have experienced has
purposefully led me to
this present moment.*

The Unconscious

I accept the unconscious part of my being.
We experience duality here on Earth. Light
and shadow exist as opposites of the
same thing.
As I expand my conscious awareness, I
shine the light of awareness into the
unconscious part of my being.
This transforms my fear of the darkness and
unknown into the light of understanding
and awareness.
As I progress on my spiritual journey, I grow
into the light.

*I accept the parts of me that are
unconscious. As I shine the light of
awareness into the shadow part of me,
I transcend my fear .*

Spiritual Teachers

I pay attention to how information
   resonates within me to know if a teacher
   is right for me.
Teachers can come in the form of authors,
   therapists, ministers, gurus, and friends.
If I feel free and closer to knowing my true
   Self, then a teacher is good for me.
I evaluate my reactions, body feelings, and
   thoughts when I am with a teacher.
This takes me closer to God and wholeness.

*I attract a teacher that resonates
with me.*

Anger

I stop fearing other people's anger.

My inner child may feel scared and want to take responsibility when another person erupts, but the adult within me is strong now and able to talk to and soothe the fear of my inner child.

I see angry people as being in pain and scapegoating responsibility for their pain.

I detach from taking responsibility for other people's anger.

I own my own anger and process it without blaming and hurting others.

I take responsibility for feeling only my own anger.

My Body

I am worthy of having a beautiful physical
   form and presence.
My thoughts direct my body.
I pay attention to mixed messages I send
   my body.
I give it clear, loving, reasonable, and
   achievable directions.
My body wants to please me.
My body knows how to balance itself and
   communicates with me when it needs
   something such as exercise or stretching
   or fasting.
I listen when my body talks.

I love my body and my body loves me.

Food

I thank my food for nourishing and building
my body.
My body is in charge of directing the food.
If I should eat something I believe is bad
and will, for example, make me fat, then
I change my thinking.
My body knows how to turn up the
thermostat to metabolize excess food if I
believe this is so.

*Food is my friend. I bless the food that
I eat and let my body process it for my
highest good.*

Opening

I open my heart today to feel all the good
in my life.

I am the gatekeeper and can close the
gate, if I choose, in situations that are
beyond my ability.

Eventually, I will open to all and not be
susceptible to being hurt or angered by
other people and situations.

Today, I appreciate what is good and
loving in my life.

I open the gate to my heart to this love and
goodness.

*I open my heart to love and support in
my life.*

Compassion

I am connected to all people everywhere.
I have loving compassion for all the people
    of the world.
I send love to others who I do not know
    personally, so they will progress on their
    journey in this life.
Suffering or undergoing life's challenges is
    made easier with the loving compassion
    of others.
I have a kind thought, word, or action for all
    the people in my life today.
I extend my love by having compassion for
    people today.

*I live my life with loving compassion
for all others.*

Animals

I appreciate the animal kingdom.
I learn a lot about myself by watching animals.
I communicate with an animal today in order to experience the blending of my consciousness with another living being.
As I observe a pet, a bird, or squirrel, I imagine what they are thinking and feeling.
It comforts me to spend time being with animals.

I experience communion with an animal to learn about myself and exchange love.

Wholeness

I remember to see my wholeness rather
   than to dwell on the challenges that a
   part of me experiences.
I center myself continually.
I release the importance of the drama in
   my life.
The main focus of my day is my wholeness.

I am whole and complete right now.

Plants

I love and appreciate the beauty that
plants bring to my life.
They nurture and soothe me when I am
stressed.
A walk among greenery calms and
balances me.
I practice extending my consciousness to a
plant or tree in order to feel its
consciousness.

*I spend time with plants and trees and
flowers to balance my emotions and
blend consciousness.*

Sunlight

I receive the energy of the sun today.
I spend a few moments in sunlight to
    experience the full spectrum of light,
    which is necessary for my health.
I appreciate the process of photosynthesis
    which allows me to consume the energy
    of the sun in the form of plants I eat and
    to breathe in energy from the air.
My life is made possible from the energy of
    the sun.

*I live in gratitude for the light the sun
shines on me.*

Balance

I live my life with balance.
I pay attention to any part of me that needs
help whether it be physical, emotional,
mental, or spiritual.
I correct anything that does not support my
balance.
I notice what keeps me in alignment and
remember to make these things a habit
in my life.

*I balance myself physically,
emotionally, mentally, and spiritually.*

Peace

I create inner peace in my life.
I focus on meeting my inner needs so I can
    enjoy peace in my outer world.
Peaceful thoughts and words to myself
    dissolve my conflicts.
As I meet others, I silently greet them by
    affirming, "Peace be with you."
For at least a moment, they feel my energy
    as a mirror of calm peace.

*I live from the place of peace within me
and reflect it to all others I meet.*

Color

I use color in my environment and clothing
to influence my emotional body.
I notice the colors that balance me and
help me change patterns and habits.
If, for example, I easily scatter my energy
and move too quickly, I am expressing
warm colors of reds and oranges and
yellows.
Being around cool colors of blues, greens,
and violets would help me create a
balance.

*I am like an artist painting with a full
palette of colors in my life.*

Giving

I choose to give my energy where it is
    needed.
I allow myself to recognize the difference
    between people who need nurturing
    from me and those who refuse to learn to
    nurture themselves.
Those who need to learn self-nurturance
    benefit from my encouragement and
    not from my doing it for them.
I teach self-nurturing by modeling it and not
    by creating dependency.
If I choose to get involved with those who
    are "using" me, then I need to establish a
    fair exchange of energy.
I may, for example, charge for my services.

*I give nurturing freely to those in need;
I remember to recognize
unhealthy dependency.*

Assignment

I am a part of the Greater Whole; I am a
    necessary cell in the larger body called
    God or the Universe.
 Without me, the Universe would not be
    complete.
I accept the assignment to be uniquely me.
I love and accept myself right now, this
    moment, and choose to complete my
    mission.

I accept my mission to be uniquely me.

Reawakening

I am reawakening to who I already am.
I no longer allow the early conditioning of
    my childhood to hold me back from the
    awareness of my goodness.
I willingly cooperate to express more and
    more the innate goodness that is within
    me.
I accept the process of pain, struggle, and
    disappointment to quicken within me the
    light of understanding.
I release all feelings of unworthiness.

*I reawaken to the awareness that I am
a part of God in physical expression.*

Vessel

My body is a vessel for Spirit.

It is my privilege to be a channel for the love and light of Spirit to use my talents and gifts in service of goodwill.

It is a great opportunity to be alive at this dynamic period in time and to know that I am a living unit of God.

I thank each cell in my body for living its purpose in order to give me a physical vehicle to be used as a perfect vessel for Spirit.

I am a perfect vessel for the Higher Will of Spirit to use in service to humanity.

Healing Relationships

It is time to be friends and to drop the
   facade of not caring and not trusting.
I choose to make peace and drop the
   script that makes another the "bad guy."
I release my resentments from the past.
I accept and support others to be who they
   are and to do what they need to do.
I choose to see others' good qualities.
May the peace of understanding come to
   each of us as we forgive ourselves and
   each other.

I face the future as a friend to all.

Critical Mass

I am more conscious than unconscious
  now.
The inner battle is over as the critical mass
  for consciousness and light has been
  reached.
Life is much easier now.
I continue to heal any dark places in my
  consciousness that hook me into
  unhealthy attachment.
I march to the beat of the rhythm of my
  own soul now.

The critical mass has been reached;
I live from the Light of my Soul.

Relating with Feeling

My conflicts with others dissipate as I relate on a feeling level.
I hear the feelings behind others' words. I notice body language.
My power increases as I slow my reactions, and I stop telling, advising, and trying to fix others.
Instead, I allow others to drink from the oasis of my cool, clear, refreshing water of consciousness as I relate on a feeling level.

I relate on a feeling level with others.

Inner Vision

In order to see with my inner eyes, I release
my judgments.

I let go of the polarity of beauty and
harshness.

I see them as complimentary and not as
opposites.

The inner vision I had as a child returns to
me now.

I concern myself with living in the Now; I do
not look too far into the future or rehash
the past.

I have the patience to see the beauty of
each experience.

*My inner vision returns as I concern
myself with the process of now; I let go
of judgments and develop patience.*

Adventure

Life is an adventure, and I explore
uncharted territory.
Today, I choose an area to explore that is
outside of my normal boundaries.
I may explore something on the physical
level such as, walking in the wilderness or
signing up for a karate class.
I may explore emotionally by joining a
support group or taking a class on
psychodrama, or I can explore mentally
by reading a book outside my usual area
of interest or belief system.
I can be a pioneer in consciousness by
meditating.

*I see my life as an adventure with more
and more to explore and experience.*

Spontaneity

I listen to my inner child today and live with
    spontaneity.
Rather than get bogged down with my
    lessons in self-discipline and responsibility,
    I choose to be more spontaneous.
Those sudden moments that allow me to
    exchange a smile with a salesperson or a
    janitor or a child or a passerby are
    enjoyed.
The brief connections of the heart are felt
    everywhere I go today.

I lighten up and live with spontaneity.

Excitement

I allow myself to feel excited today.
Somewhere within me I know what is joyful
    to experience or express.
I can anticipate my new life unfolding when
    I live in a state of expanded
    consciousness.
I am excited about my new awareness
    even when I have challenges.
I am excited to discover how to live in the
    world and not get caught in the illusions
    or problems of the world.

*I am excited about my life and choose
to live from expanded consciousness.*

Enlightenment

I am in the process of "lightening" my
consciousness.
I see that I go through doorways that bring
me more and more understanding.
I experience a certain degree of
enlightenment right now.
I trust the process of the Universe and know I
will progress towards total enlightenment
when the lessons are learned.
I share the light that I now possess with
others.

The journey of enlightenment is
progressing well in my life.

My Rights

I have the right to complain, to return purchases to stores, or to write letters to managers when I do not receive proper goods or services.

When I pay for something, I have the right to have things work.

I can assert myself without being aggressive and hurtful.

I communicate openly and honestly to handle corrections in goods and services not correctly provided.

I assert myself when my rights are violated. I know I can take care of myself and receive what I pay for.

Loving Myself

I am responsible for loving myself.
I do not expect others to meet my needs.
I enjoy it when another can give me love,
   attention, and support.
When I become dependent on another
   and expect them to do for me what I
   cannot do for myself, I set myself up for
   disappointment.
I always return to the source of my being to
   love and care for myself.
I practice healing meditations with my inner
   child when I become too needy.
This reparenting by the Inner Self helps me
   to love myself in my day-to-day living.

I take responsibility for loving myself.

Looking Within

I look within to find my True Self.
My Spiritual Self reveals itself more and more
as I learn to go within in meditation,
contemplation, and journal writing.
As I question my reasons for acting a certain
way and my reasons for everything I do, I
am learning to tell the difference
between my conditioned personality
and my True Self.
It feels good to get to know and express my
True Self.

I look within to find my True Self.

Enough

I am enough by myself.
I do not need other people to make me
   whole.
I continue to work on loving myself
   completely.
As I learn to fill myself with love, I have no
   missing pieces that are dependent on
   other people to fulfill.
I am joyful knowing I can handle whatever
   may challenge my security today
   because I know that I am strong within.

*I am enough because I know how to
love myself.*

Inner Guidance

I listen to my inner guidance; it continually shows me the way out of the maze of illusion.

I spend enough time with myself to learn the difference between the control of the little self and wisdom of the Higher Self.

My inner wisdom can guide me better than I ever thought possible.

I see the goodness I experience when I release my outer drama and accept my inner guidance.

I listen to my inner guidance.

Power

I have the power to create my life the way I
    want.
The source of my power is my Spiritual Self
    which is linked to God.
I align my personality self with my Spiritual
    Self, and the energy flows easily.
I am clear in my mind what I want to
    create.
I visualize and affirm it, and then I allow the
    Universe to draw it to me.
I can create whatever I am able to accept.

*I accept the power to create what serves
my highest good.*

My Father

I honor the man who is or was my father in
    life.
He played an important role for my life
    script.
I send him love and peace to help him
    grow further on his journey.
I release any residue of anger or hurt for
    unmet expectations.
I internalize from this man the qualities I
    need for my inner father.
Any missing qualities I need, I create myself.

(This passage may be read on
your father's birthday.)

I am a good father to my inner child.

Earth

I honor the earth and all she provides.
This unique planet loves and supports me.
I, in turn, take care of her.
I express gratitude for living on such a
    beautiful planet where I may see colors,
    trees, flowers, animals, water, mountains,
    and clouds.

I love the Earth and the Earth loves me.

Grounding

I feel the energy of the earth support me.
I stand with my feet in contact with the
ground and visualize energy coming up
from the earth.
This energy connects me in a solid way with
this physical dimension.
I easily move around in my body.
I live safely and consciously.

*My feet ground me to the earth which
supports me in this world.*

Judgments from Others

Today, I detach from the judgments of
   others.
I make my own decisions based on the
   consequences I am willing to live with.
I no longer need an outside authority to tell
   me what to do.
I continue to detach from other people's
   criticism, expectations, and judgments of
   me.

*I detach from other people's
judgments of me.
I am my own authority.*

Diet

I pay attention to my diet; I eat foods that
are full of life force and that enlighten my
body.

I eat only food that is prepared in an
atmosphere of love.

I bless my food before I eat it, to purify it for
my body.

I give my gratitude to the plant and/or
animal that is serving me.

I only eat when it is calm and peaceful.

I drink plenty of water.

When I am ready to make dietary changes,
I begin gathering information about
nutrition.

*I love and nurture my body with high
vibration foods, prepared and eaten in
an atmosphere of love.*

Exercise

I keep my body in good physical shape through yoga, movement, or an exercise program.

I walk and use stairs whenever possible in order to use my physical form.

If my body is "differently abled," I create a special program for me to get maximum strength from my body.

I create a strong physical form for Spirit to live in.

My body is a vehicle for my Spiritual Self to use.

I take care of my physical body with regular exercise designed for my needs.

Acceptance

I accept, not only myself, but other people
   as well.
Each of us is doing the best we can with our
   level of awareness.
Acceptance does not mean I have to be
   around someone who hurts me because
   they are unaware.
It is simply understanding them with
   compassion.

*I accept everyone wherever they are in
their level of awareness.*

Birthday

Today is my special day.
I give thanks to the people who gave birth
to me.
I commit to loving myself from this day
forward.
As I look in the mirror today, I say supportive,
kind things to myself. I listen to my Inner
Self.
I celebrate my day and am not dependent
on others to make it my special day.
I treat myself to small, nurturing gifts.

(Exchange this passage with your birthday.)

I celebrate myself today.

Traits

My traits are neutral; they become positive
or negative depending upon how I use
them.

I make a list of my traits and use neutral
words to describe them.

All negative traits have a positive
compliment.

For example, my trait of codependency is
the ability to respond to others with the
intention of helping them.

I choose to get in touch with the positive
use of my traits.

*I accept my unique set of personality
traits. They are me, and
I express them positively.*

Service

I dedicate my life to serving others.
Once I have a good sense of myself, my
　　needs, and how to nurture myself, I give
　　my talents and time to making this world
　　a better place.
I do not get hooked into giving to every
　　person and cause that crosses my path.
I discriminate between those who
　　compliment my need to give and those
　　who drain my energy.
I have the ability to say "No" to people and
　　causes that do not match up with my
　　choice of service.

*I choose a life of service and give from
my overflow.*

True Nurturing

I am the catalyst for others to have a
     greater sense of themselves.
I know when to ignite the inner fire of
     another and when to let go and watch
     the kindled fire begin to blaze on its own.
True nurturing comes from helping others to
     discover their own ability to maintain the
     fire.
I encourage others to do what I have
     learned to do for myself.

*I nurture others by recognizing those
who need my spark and those who
simply need encouragement to develop
and sustain their own flame.*

My Importance

My life is important and is much more than
 my little self can understand.

It is as if my soul were part of a double helix
 in a DNA molecule.

Half of the chain is already in existence as
 an expression of the creative Source; my
 life then mirrors a small piece of the
 chain.

It is comforting for me to know that there is
 a bigger, well-thought-out plan for my life
 to follow and that I am not blindly
 stumbling along.

I dedicate my life to discovering and
 exploring my purpose.

*I feel the importance of my special,
unique life.*

Being Stuck

I am in the perfect place on my spiritual
path at all times.
I let go of the moments when I do not feel
the light of understanding or forget to
take care of myself or forget what I knew
yesterday.
Even when I feel stuck, I observe my actions
and feelings unemotionally.
If what I am doing is not working, I need to
turn in another direction.
I forgive myself for being stuck; it is part of
the process.

When stuck, I look in another direction.

The Way

There is only one way out of my problems,
   dilemmas, and pain.
The way is to live Love... give Love, receive
   Love, express Love, and be Love.
As I allow the Higher Power to use me as a
   channel for unconditional Love, then my
   way is illumined.

I live the way of Love.

My Selves

At times, I feel as if I have different people
living inside of me.

Some do not cooperate, some are wise,
and some are immature.

It is my job to direct these different aspects
of myself to work together.

I facilitate the polar opposites within me; for
example, I have the destructive part and
the helping part talk and listen to each
other.

To deny or suppress a part is to create a
roadblock on the path.

This roadblock could come in the form of
an illness, an accident, or a person
mirroring a suppressed aspect of myself.

*I listen to all parts of myself in order to
heal and grow into a mature adult.*

Positive Intentions

Each immature aspect of me has a positive
　　intention.
As I discover the positive intention, I can
　　thank that part of me for the job it has
　　been doing.
Then, I can talk to it expressing that I want
　　to go beyond this present attitude or
　　behavior to something more mature.
I continue to communicate with this part of
　　me until this immature aspect is willing to
　　cooperate and grow to maturity.
I have the ability to heal immature aspects
　　of my character with this inner dialogue
　　process.

I release immature aspects of myself.

Greater Meaning

I have a choice in how I experience the
   things that happen in my day.
I am learning to totally live from my Higher
   Self and let the Will of Heaven express
   through me.
I do not judge experiences as good or bad.
I look for greater meaning in all the difficult
   things I undergo.
This greater meaning improves the quality
   of my journey.

*I choose to look for greater meaning as
I walk through challenging situations.*

Co-creating

I am connected to all other humans in this
experience of life on this planet.

If I do not like or understand situations that
present themselves in my life, I remember
that we are all learning to be what we
already are...One.

Confusion dissipates when I remember to
co-create reality rather than force my will
or allow another to force their will on me.

I am responsible for part of the outcomes
that manifest when other people are
involved.

Creating reality is shared with others.

I view life from the perspective of co-creating. When two or more of us come together, we share responsibility for creating reality.

Quality of the Journey

I am responsible for my interpretation of
　　events that occur in my day.
The quality of my journey is up to me.
I can choose to suffer and get distracted by
　　pain, or I can stay centered and
　　conscious while undergoing challenging
　　lessons.
As I see the big picture, I discover that I no
　　longer need to suffer.
I improve the quality of my life by my
　　interpretation of events that come my
　　way.

*I improve the quality of my journey by
staying conscious and seeing the
patterns of the big picture.*

Patterns

I recognize the negative patterns I learned
from my family of origin that repeat
themselves in relationships at work and at
home.
I transform my current relationship problems
by first seeing the patterns and then
spending time pondering the choices I
have to break out of these patterns.
I attract healthy people and patterns of
relating when I work on myself first.
I am no longer an unconscious victim.

*I am healing the limiting, crystallized
patterns from the past by working on
my awareness and pondering my choices.*

Improving

My life is improving day by day.
I apply my newly awakened consciousness
    to life situations.
I see things differently and make new
    choices.
I see the progress I have made and am
    joyfully accepting of myself.
The birth of my new self is steadily
    progressing.
I am optimistic about the future.
I work on today and live it to the fullest.
Tomorrow takes care of itself.
I am peaceful and relaxed as my life
    unfolds.

*Day by day, I see my life improving. I
celebrate the changes I am making and
the peace I am experiencing now.*

Mastering

I am the master of my life.

I take responsibility for my life.

It is no longer a crisis if I make a mistake or a "wrong" choice.

I will pay the consequences of my choices and release any critical judgments from my inner self-talk.

As I grow more aware each day, I realize all that I have mastered in my life so far.

I continue to step into today to master what presents itself to me.

I am the master of my life.

Double Agent

I am a double agent.
I live my life from the place of expanded
    awareness; I willingly live in the world.
I can see the patterns and reasons behind
    circumstances that affect my life and do
    not get caught in the drama.
Instead, I tune into my spiritual presence
    and know I am achieving wholeness; it is
    only a matter of time before I am totally
    released from the unpleasant patterns.
I participate in life sharing my new
    awareness only when appropriate.
It is okay that I am aware and that many
    others in my life are not.

*I am a double agent for the Source. I
live love without expecting others to
acknowledge me or understand me.*

Teachers

I see a lesson in every experience,
    especially the ones that are
    uncomfortable.
Each person reflects something about me
    that helps transform my consciousness.
I am also the teacher for others, whether
    they realize it or not.
I watch the dance between myself and
    others.

*I am open and observant to catch the
subtle meaning in all my interactions
with all my teachers.*

Creating as a Process

I create my experiences by seeing my life as
   a process.
I stay open to all situations and experiences
   as I go through my day.
I see detours that take me off my intended
   course as challenges to learn and grow.
Sometimes the rerouting gives me
   possibilities for greater growth than might
   have been otherwise.

*I create my day by seeing the process of
change as welcome and to be expected.*

Nurturing Myself

I go within to observe and assess my needs
   in the four areas of myself: physical,
   emotional, mental, and spiritual.
I release the blocks preventing me from
   determining my needs.
I am an adult now, and it is okay to say
   what I need and want.
I am worthy of getting my needs met.
I am no longer dependent upon others to
   meet my true needs.
In my journal, I list all the needs I am
   conscious of right now in order to begin
   the process of meeting these needs.

*I am worthy of getting my real needs
met. I go within to find out how to
nurture myself.*

Wholeness

My wholeness grows day by day.
No one has to know how deeply I am
    transforming.
If a close friend or family member notices
    that is fine; however, I do not expect
    others to follow my growth.
I share my journey only with others who are
    on a similar path.

I live from my place of wholeness.

Wounds

I continue to heal the wounds from times
　　when I was less aware.
I no longer blame others who were unable
　　to love and nurture me.
At this moment in time, I acknowledge
　　myself for all that it took to get me here.
I am here, now, healing and recovering,
　　and that is what is important.

*I release past times that wounded me.
I live in the present moment.*

Recovery

I realize it takes time to recover from the
wounds of the past.
I accept the process of recovery.
I allow fellow travelers to show me the way
when I wander or stray off my path to
recovery.

*I take one step at a time on my path
to recovery.*

Anger

I feel my anger and use its energy to make
   changes and not to blame or hurt myself
   or others.
Choices that I made or others' made
   cannot be changed in the past.
I can use this information, however, to
   create different outcomes today.
I allow the anger to come up and wash
   over my body.
I may need to exercise in order to positively
   use energy created by my anger.

*I listen to my anger, and I use its power
to make positive changes.*

Outer Appearances

I go beyond outer appearances.
I may allow others' behavior to affect me
    until I realize that I have a choice.
Instead of judging another's actions, I look
    within and identify the qualities in me
    that are being reflected.
I cannot attract anything that is not inside
    of me.
The outer reflection allows me to see what is
    disowned within myself.
I use the outer appearances or unconscious
    parts of myself to tell me what I need to
    work on.

I no longer am deceived by outer appearances; I recognize them as parts of myself.

Polarities Within

I notice polarities within myself.

These opposites give me the challenge to
learn moderation and blending.

I am a soul experiencing life for growth and
self-awareness in a system of opposites
and dualities.

Wholeness is a paradox of being both parts
of a polarity at the expense of neither.

I accept the opposite parts of myself.

I use the different aspects of myself wisely.

I balance polarities within myself.

Releasing Tension

If I have a clash of wills with other people or
a clash with my own inner polarities, I
release tension by crying, making loud
sounds, exercising, clarifying my
thoughts, journal writing, or talking.
It is similar to the calm after a thunderstorm
when a new beginning presents itself.

*I clear emotional tension when it arises
so I can clear away the old and
begin anew.*

Balance

When I do not feel a sense of balance
within myself, I calmly center myself and
allow the parts of me that need
balancing to blend.
I experience the ups and downs of life and
at the same time maintain my balance.
Like a scale, I move my outer self to
balance the Inner Self.
I am both the Inner Self and the outer self.

*I am balanced and centered as
I experience life.*

Daily Purpose

Today, I live my purpose.
Whatever presents itself to me is what I
    choose to work on.
Rather than wonder what the future
    purpose is, I focus on today.
My purpose may or may not look divine and
    holy; it may look mundane at times.
Going to work or raising a child may be part
    of the plan.
I continue to make myself a better person.
Step by step, I walk the path that is my life.
I am my purpose.

*I feel the purpose of each experience in
my day.*

Choices

I honor the choices my soul made for me to physically experience in my life.

The things that I do not like, I realize, are part of the plan for my life.

I consciously work with all aspects of my life even those that I cannot change and must accept.

I no longer fight the purpose of this life I am living.

I see the Light of Spirit behind the experiences.

Joy spreads over me every time I remember who I really am: a part of the Source growing and transforming.

I honor the choices my soul set in motion for my unfolding of consciousness.

Equilibrium

I move forward with the equilibrium of
   balanced motion just as a bird does
   when it moves its wings in flight.
This motion of balancing action with
   nurturing myself gives me the momentum
   to continue my spiritual journey.
Less effort is needed to move when I
   maintain my equilibrium.
I do all the things that nurture me so that I
   maintain this perpetual motion.

*I easily move forward on the spiritual
path by balancing my actions with
things that nurture me.*

Change

I accept that I am in an ever-changing world.

I connect to Spirit and earth at the same time by visualizing a shaft of light coming from Spirit down through the top of my head, down my spine, and into the center of the earth.

As new experiences continually move into my frame of reference,

I maintain this connection moving forward into a more wondrous experience of my Self.

Change is my friend when I connect to Spirit and matter simultaneously.

Spirit and Matter

I am a unique and incredible being; I am a combination of spirit and matter.

I am a beam of light—a particle and a wave all at the same time.

I am an extension of the Source living in a physical world.

I am also living in emotional, mental, and spiritual worlds.

I have vehicles for all the dimensions of my Self.

I am a unique blend of Spirit and matter.

Thoughts

I listen to my negative self-talk, change
them into positive statements, and write
them in my journal.

As a healing treatment for my
consciousness, I read these aloud to
myself.

I will continue to read these aloud until I feel
the real truth of my being.

My new thoughts guide me.

If I begin the negative self-talk, the new
thoughts override.

This is reprogramming my subconscious
mind.

This is like putting a new data base into a
computer.

*I put new healthy thoughts into my
mind overriding the old programming.*

Inner Child

I have the power to change the negative
    effects from my past.
I reconnect with my inner child
    communicating with loving and kind
    words.
Each day, I ask my child what he/she needs
    and wants.
If, for example, my inner child is feeling
    lonely and withdrawn, I may rock him/her
    and listen to inspiring music.
I am always ready to listen to the needs of
    my inner child.
I no longer ignore those needs or expect
    anyone else to meet them.

*I am responsible for meeting the needs
of my inner child.*

Tolerance

I am tolerant of people who are less aware than I am.

I practice forgiving them for offensive behavior and continue to love them at the impersonal level of mind (this is unconditional love that the Greeks call Agape love.)

I, however, make sure I do not set myself up to be a scapegoat or target.

I consciously decide what I can handle and what I cannot.

I do not have to continue relating in the same way if I am not taking care of myself.

I tolerate people with offensive behavior. I figure out the best plan for me to take care of myself.

Strength

I am strong.
My inner strength allows me to learn from
   whatever happens to me.
It protects me in situations where my
   awareness is limited.
I have the power to take care of myself and
   transform any dark corners that surprise
   me.
I continue my growth and unfoldment
   knowing my strength of character will
   take care of me.

I have inner strength to meet the
challenges in my life.

Beauty

I have an inner beauty that radiates and
shines on all who come onto my path.

I allow this inner beauty to penetrate my
emotional body.

It feels good to have this strength of inner
character.

I claim my power to radiate this inner light
of beauty.

*I am a beautiful expression of the
Godforce. I radiate love and beauty on
all who come into my life.*

Courage

I have the courage to move forward on the
path of life.

I am powerful because I know and feel my
inner beauty and light.

I meet life with the assurance that all is well
and is unfolding for a greater reason and
purpose.

I trust the process and have the courage to
go into my life fully experiencing all that
life has to offer.

*I have the courage to be who I am and
to experience all that my soul has in
mind for me.*

Abundance

The Universe is unlimited; thus I am able to get my needs met.

Conflicting guiding beliefs and needs within me, however, might make it appear that I am not getting what I ask for.

The most dominant need or belief wins when two are in conflict.

It is never Source that deprives me; I do it to myself by having faulty beliefs and false information on how things work.

I can only attract things in the outer world based on my level of awareness.

The Creative Source is within me and wants to move me into greater experiences of abundance.

Today, I change at least one unhealthy thought pattern to allow me to receive abundance on the mental plane so that I can manifest it on the physical plane.

I correct false feliefs so that I can have the abundance I deserve.

Materializing

I have the power to materialize what I want.

I am specific about what I want and focus my mind on it.

As I focus, I begin drawing what I want towards me.

I pay attention to all negative thoughts that tell me I do not deserve or cannot have what I want.

I talk back to this voice with words such as, "I deserve to have a loving relationship," or "I do not have to be perfect to be worthy of love."

Once I get clear on what it is I want and change my negative self-talk, I let go, and the universe brings it to me in correct timing.

I am powerful and materialize what I want and deserve.

Divine Success

I listen to Spirit when I am creating.
I choose to manifest only what is loving and
of service to myself or others.
I am successful when I create in
accordance with my spiritual nature.
Will guided by Spirit brings the ideas of Spirit
into physical reality.
I spend time meditating and concentrating
on the true meaning of success, and I
manifest what my Higher Self has in mind
for me.

I create divine success in my life.

Heart

My heart opens to the love of Spirit.
It gives me the support I need to heal the
　　ruptures in my close relationships.
As I fill myself with the love of Spirit, I am
　　renewed and face the difficulties that
　　need to be resolved and dissolved.
New patterns of wholeness emerge with the
　　opening of my heart center.

*I open my heart to the love and support
of Spirit.*

Letting Go

I leap into the unknown assured of my
　　success because of the Light I possess.
I trust by letting go of the unreal in my life;
　　reality will support me.
If others see me as a fool, I remember how I
　　judged others when I was not mature
　　enough in consciousness to understand.
Rather than convince or prove my choices,
　　I quietly progress on the path of
　　enlightenment.
I no longer need loved ones to understand
　　my process or come along with me.
I let go of everything that is not in rhythm
　　with my true destiny.

*I let go of everything that holds me in
bondage to what I am not.*

Magic of Spirit

I live with the magic of Spirit.
My life is a channel for this energy.
I simply allow it to flow through me.
I live by letting go moment by moment.
I experience the guidance of the Higher
    Power.
Sometimes this magic is a feeling; at other
    times, it is a vision or a silent voice within.

*I dance with the guidance of the
magical energy of Spirit.*

Secrets

I joyfully hold the secrets of wisdom within me.

As I progress on the path of wholeness, I experience more and more of what is already inside me.

My intellect works with my intuition. I need both parts of my mind.

My inner wisdom is understood and put into words with the help of my analytical mind.

My Inner Self has all the wisdom to guide my life. I tune into the secrets of this inner wisdom.

Body

My body is healthy and whole.
Each organ and cell works harmoniously as
a team player with all other parts of my
body.
I appreciate all the physical parts of me
and the good job that each part does to
sustain me.
I tune into my body to find places in need.
I send love and light to any part of my
system that is hurting.

My body is healthy and whole.

Creativity

I allow my natural creativity to flow through
me.
I connect with my Higher Self through
meditation.
Then I use my power of affirmation and
visualization to manifest in the physical as
Spirit has guided me.
I express the Love of God when I allow the
creative Spirit to flow through me.

**I allow the Spirit of creativity to flow
through me.**

Tradition

I honor the traditions of my family and
   culture.
I participate to the degree that it feels right
   to me.
I use the routine of traditions to order my life.
Traditions anchor me to my past and
   provide secure roots.
I evaluate what I want to carry forward in
   my life from all the traditions presented to
   me.

*I feel safe by honoring and practicing
the traditions that support me in my life.*

Authority

I respect the authority of people in power
  who use their power for the greater good
  of others.
I notice those who do not have the ability
  to lead others and who misuse their
  power and authority.
I am conscious of my own authority and
  how I affect others.
I am aware of the higher authority I receive
  from the Higher Power.

*I listen to the authority of my Higher
Self when I am in positions
of power and authority.*

Union

I accept the union of Spirit and matter into
    my body awareness.
When I am in this place of grace, I love
    each person unconditionally.
My special love relationships work easily
    when I remember all that I am.
As the superconscious mind of the Source
    enfolds me, the conscious and
    subconscious parts of my mind are free
    of separation.
I join all parts of me in oneness.

*I am at one with all that I am, and I
experience union within myself.*

Higher Self

I live my day feeling safe, secure, and
    connected with my Higher Self.
I allow my Greater Self to be in charge of
    my life.
Inner and outer conflicts, as well as physical
    and emotional addictions, no longer rule
    my life.
My Spiritual Self takes charge of my
    personality problems, and I easily live
    with peace and harmony.

I turn my life over to my Higher Self.

Friendship

I care about my friends.
I appreciate the unconditional love and
emotional support of my close friends.
I express gratitude to those who have
shared my pain, sadness, joy, and
excitement.
I send love to people who have shared my
life with me.

*I appreciate my friends. I lift them into
the Light.*

Purpose

I know I have a purpose.
I am ready to remove the fear of having this
    purpose revealed to me.
I have worked diligently on healing my
    consciousness and am now ready to
    move forward to serve others.
I bring my gift of wholeness into my day and
    into my interactions with others.
I am ready to receive the next part of my
    spiritual purpose.

*I am open to receiving my next
assignment from Spirit.*

Goodness

Good things are happening in my life.
I watch as my life unfolds with more and
more goodness each day.
I release old hurts and pains, and goodness
finds its way onto my path.
I focus my mind on what is happening in my
day that is good.

*I receive the goodness that I deserve in
my life.*

Death

I honor the time I have on earth today.
I see that the fear of death stops me from a
   true experience of the present.
I allow my fears of death to melt into the
   experiences ahead of me today.
I am alive right now and cherish my life.
I accept that death affects only the
   physical aspects of me.
In Spirit there is no death.

*I embrace the time that I have right
now for loving and learning.*

Transformation

I accept change in my life.
I let go when I reach the place of not
    knowing.
I let go of old patterns and behaviors in
    order to transform aspects of myself into
    greater and greater wholeness.
I am like the caterpillar who is changing into
    a butterfly.

*The power of transformation is active
in my life.*

The Golden Mean

I live my life with the intention to experience
whatever comes my way.

I no longer avoid the positive or negative
experiences that are presented to me.

I am healing all the misperceptions,
judgments, and beliefs that took me
away from the middle path of quiet,
calm, and peace.

As I trust my process, I choose to experience
the place of balance that the ancient
Greeks called The Golden Mean.

I am no longer seduced into the highs or
lows.

I live joyfully from my heart.

I trust the process.

By living with inner balance and calm,
I experience the Golden Mean.

Intuition

I act on my intuition, and divine order
   appears in my life.
When I center myself and listen to the quiet,
   still voice from within, I have all of the
   protection and guidance necessary.
I hear this silent voice whenever I ask for
   help.

*I am protected and guided by the power
of intuition.*

Timing

With my inner growth and expansion, I am
aware of the proper timing for me.

I continue to release expectations that are
no longer realistic for me.

I can only respond from my present level of
awareness.

I honor my emotional needs, and I travel at
a comfortable rate along my path.

My goals unfold at the perfect rate for me.

I manage my time and allow my Self to
open like a flower blooming at its perfect
time.

*I respond to the proper timing for me to
open and grow.*

Goals

I know the difference between my goals
and the journey of meeting these goals.
I enjoy the process of life as I meet my
goals.
I evaluate my goals to see if I have
outgrown any that were sent forth in less
aware days.
I take the risks appropriate for today.
I move forward with awareness and self-
assurance to meet my goals.

*I clearly see and enjoy the journey of
meeting my goals.*

Gardener

I plant new seed thoughts in the garden of
   my mind.
I pull the weed thoughts that interfere with
   my growth.
With loving care, I nurture the new seeds as
   they grow into full stature and beauty
   which reflects the blossoming of Spirit
   within me.

I am the gardener of my consciousness.

Victory

I celebrate the achievements that I
   accomplish.
I rest for a time after reaching a goal in
   order to assimilate the total experience.
I enjoy my process of achieving.
I know when to do and when to be.

*I find joy in the creative process; I
enjoy both the doing and the being.*

Regeneration

I am regenerating my whole being.
As my consciousness changes, all the cells
in my body get a boost.
Emotionally, I process all of the old stored
energy of pain and fear in order to
release me from the bondage of
physical hurting.
I choose to look straight into old patterns of
pain and fear, to release them, and to
regenerate my total self.

I am regenerating my total being.

Others' Choices

I stop controlling other people's choices.
I allow them their learning experiences
through their achievements, mistakes,
and experimentations.
I maintain my inner peace when a loved
one chooses options I deem negative.
I return my focus to myself each time I get
too involved with another person's
choices.

*I focus on my life and allow others to
make their own choices.*

Emotional Pain

I no longer criticize myself when I repeat a
   negative-feeling emotional pattern.
I realize the repetition allows the intensity to
   register an unconscious pattern in my
   conscious awareness.
Once emotional pain registers, my mental
   self can gather information and try new
   things to eliminate the old pattern.
My mental self breaks the emotional prisons
   I have created.

---

*I choose new ideas and thoughts to
break my patterns of emotional pain.*

Harmlessness

I practice harmlessness by living my life
without being hurtful to myself or others in
all that I think, say, and do.
I choose to live from the place of right
thinking and right action by listening to
my heart at all times.

I live my life with harmlessness.

Contentment

I am content to be who I am and where I
am at this moment.
This does not stop my growth; the process of
living with goals and achievements
continues.
I take the time, however, to experience the
joy of all that I have accomplished up to
this moment.
I am content.

I am content in this moment.

Innate Abilities

I acknowledge my innate abilities and
    talents that are to be developed and
    eventually shared.
My special abilities no longer have to stay
    hidden.
It is never too late to begin appreciating my
    gifts.
I look at what I have that is unique.
It does not have to be what traditionally is
    appreciated by society, and it does not
    have to bring in income.
Developing my special abilities fills me with
    joy and rounds out my total being.

*I develop my special abilities and
talents with the sole purpose of
rounding out my consciousness.*

Family

I appreciate my family.

I look realistically at this group and accept
what cannot be changed.

I relate to each member individually and
remove myself from conflicts between
other members.

I am only responsible for myself in relation to
each member individually.

I am brave about bringing up issues that
need clarification and healing.

I move in the direction of healthy, loving
relationships with all my family members.

*I am part of a family. I appreciate this
group and my relationship to each
person in the group.*

Roles

I look at the roles I play in my family, at
   work, and in my close relationships.
I reassess these roles.
Do I want to continue them?
Are any unhealthy for me?
Do I want to create new ones or
   renegotiate old ones?
I evaluate my roles to reflect my inner
   growth at this time.

*I am conscious of the roles I play; I take
time to evaluate any changes
I need to make.*

Rules

I make a list of the rules by which I live my
    life.
I think about these rules and clarify the ones
    that need to be changed.
I eliminate the ones that are outdated and
    no longer serve me or the greater good.
In their place, I create new rules that
    support my new growth.

*I evaluate and update the rules by
which I live my life.*

Code of Conduct

I write down the code of conduct that
   guides my life.
I become clear what my values are.
I choose to live by the standards that are
   good for me.
Any part of the code that I am unable to
   adhere to is an area for further growth; it
   is the next agenda on my path.

*I live my life with a code of conduct for
my true values.*

Time

Time is my friend.
I work well with time.
I expand time by organizing what I need to
do and visualizing the most efficient way
to work.
I compress time by speeding up what I am
doing.
I use my time wisely.
I balance what I have to do with what I
want to do.
"Down" time is as important as productive
time; I live the balance of the two.

Time is my friend.

Friendship

I value my circle of friends.
I connect emotionally with my close friends.
I am there for them, and they are there for me.
I share my journey with them and listen as they share their journey with me.
Close friends provide an extra measure of support and love.
I exchange love and support with my friends.

I value my close friends and share myself with them.

Wholeness

I enjoy all of me.
I shine the light of awareness into all my
    spaces to bring any fear, shame, and
    darkness into the open light.
In the light, I heal and feel all of me.
I recognize the parts of me that still need
    attention.
I am willing to go further in my process of
    loving and accepting all that I am.
I experience wholeness when I allow myself
    to be what I am.

*I accept my whole self and know
I am good.*

Higher Will

I have the desire to be all that I truly am.
I trust turning my little will over to the Higher
Will and Power.
I am a fragment of the Greater Will and
Power.
I feel light and free when I relieve myself of
the burden of controlling all that I
experience.
I am free living from the Higher Will.

The Higher Will guides my living.

Meditation

I live in a continuous meditation.
I talk directly to my Spiritual Self which is
    connected to the Source of all.
I receive direct guidance as I allow this
    power to flow through me.
I take the time to quiet my mind and
    become open to receiving my
    guidance.

I live my day in a continuous
meditation connected to the Source.

Thankfulness

I allow myself to experience the good
feelings that come from being thankful.
Today, I list all the good things that have
happened to me, all the people I am
grateful to have in my life, and all the
awareness I have had this year.
I focus on what is working and what I do
have in my life today.
I feel the collective celebration of giving
thanks from the people in my nation.
I am a part of this group experience.

NOTE: Read this passage on
Thanksgiving Day as the date changes
each year.

I am thankful for my life and all the
opportunities I have to explore and
experience.

Stillness

I experience stillness today to know the
beauty of my soul.

I listen to the silent voice of inner spiritual
authority which guides me and shows me
the way.

Even when my outer world is hurried and
demands are placed on me, I go in
peace because I go into the quiet
stillness that is within.

In stillness, I listen to my soul.

Cooperation

I cooperate with members of my family and co-workers.

I pay attention to the larger picture; we are all souls growing in consciousness.

I do not dwell on the difficulty of others' personalities.

I see that I can make a difference.

I center myself and respond from the place of maturity.

I limit my reactions and communicate with skill and deep thought.

I cooperate with others around me.

Silence

Today, I observe my world.
I listen to others and silence my reactive
    mind.
I live with the intention of quieting my mind
    chatter and receiving the guidance my
    Higher Self has for me.
I take the time to slow myself down, to
    practice living with silence, to listen to my
    intuition, and then to act wisely.

I observe my world in silence.

Playfulness

I stop taking myself so seriously today.
I notice when I can lighten up.
I let my inner child play in situations that
    normally stress me.
I cease overworking problems that seem to
    drain me.
I open the door of creativity that was shut
    to my consciousness; I remember to play.

***I unlock the door to my creativity by
being playful.***

Partner

I appreciate my partner (this can be a love
partner, business partner, roommate,
etc.) today.
I focus on his or her good qualities.
I mirror love and kindness to my partner and
help them see their inner beauty and
light.
I verbalize my appreciation.

*I express gratitude for my
partner today.*

Codependence

I pay attention to my need to be needed.
I give because that is part of my nature and
  choose to continue giving.
I am clear, however, about my boundaries
  so that I respect my own needs and
  have the energy I need to live my life.
I clean up any relationships which have not
  supported me or in which I have placed
  other's needs before mine.
I get support from others who are also doing
  this work.
With honest communication, I confront the
  people with whom I am in a
  codependent relationship.

*I transform my codependent
relationships to healthy
interdependent relationships.*

Remembering Who I Am

I hold firmly in my mind that I am a part of
the Universe.
There is no way to stop being part of the
Grand Plan.
To experience pain at the personality level is
to grow in consciousness.
I never forget, through all my experiences,
that I am part of the Source.
Some call me a child of God, others a son
of God, and others call me a Christed
being.

*I remember who I am at all times so
that I do not buy into the illusion of
separation and confusion.*

Detachment

I watch with detachment as others express
strong emotions.

When another loses his/her temper, I watch
with curiosity trying to figure out what is
happening within that person.

I do not take it personally when another
looses his/her temper with me.

I am not the cause of such outbursts; I am
only the trigger of something much
deeper going on with him/her.

I remove myself from people who experience rage.

Communication is not possible at that time.

I visualize the other person surrounded by
light each time they come into my mind.

*I communicate with an intention of
being authentic and genuine.*

My Body

I love and accept my body.
I release the media's and other people's
images of how my body should look.
I like myself even if my body does not fit
these images set by others.
I talk to my body and tell it, "I love you and
thank you for doing what you do."
My self-esteem is not based on what appears to be assets or flaws in my body.
I do not compare or make judgments about
other people's bodies.

***I see beauty in every body,
including my own.***

Problems

I see my problems as my teachers.
When I need healing and am unaware,
these teachers present situations that
look like problems.
A problem simply means I have the
opportunity to heal the past and
become more aware.
I gently confront, ponder, and work with
what I see as problems.
I connect with my Higher Self when I need
help.
My Higher Self is bigger than any problem I
can create.

I allow my problems to be my teachers.

Understanding

I like to be understood.
I begin by clarifying my thoughts and
    feelings before I communicate with
    another.
I do this by journal writing, talking into a
    tape recorder, or talking out loud
    imagining that another person is there.
When I understand myself, I communicate
    easily with others.
I also practice understanding others.

*I understand myself, and I
communicate easily with others.*

Addictions

My addictions, whether to a person, substance, security, etc., allow me to become conscious of my blocks to wholeness.

I choose to stop judging myself for past behaviors that have allowed the blocks to continue.

I transform my addictive behavior, not through suppression, but through understanding myself and getting my needs met.

I honor feelings that were suppressed and creative energy that did not know how to express itself.

I allow my addictive behaviors to show me where I am stuck in the past. I allow suppressed parts of myself to express creatively.

Ego

I love and appreciate all that the ego (little
   self) has done to survive.
I am now ready to submit the ego to the
   direction of my Higher Self.
I choose to listen to the quiet voice of the
   Higher Power.
My Higher Self steps down the frequency of
   power so that I can sense, hear, or see
   this higher truth on a personal level.

I allow my Higher Self to rule my ego.

Senses

I honor my five senses; they help me
interact with my physical world.
I also honor my sense of intuition that goes
beyond the physical to connect me with
the world of Spirit.
I need all my senses, and they are good.

I appreciate all my senses; they help me
interact with the physical and
spiritual worlds.

Manifestation

I am capable of manifesting what I need
and want.
The better I know myself, the wiser I create.
I go within to determine what the true
desire is, and then I visualize and affirm
myself manifesting on the physical level.
I feel very deeply the nature of what I want
to create in order to add power to the
creating.
Then, I am able to let go and allow the
Universe to determine the proper timing
and way of manifesting what I want.

I manifest what is wise and good for me.

Taming My Mind

I master the thoughts and images in my
    mind.
I pay attention to what I am thinking and
    picturing so that I can choose to create
    my highest good.
I focus on the thoughts and pictures that
    support my healing and release those
    that keep me stuck in the past.
I continue to train my mind to be here now,
    without judgment, but with love and
    support.

*I tame my mind in order to create my
highest good and demonstrate
my wholeness.*

Patience

I cooperate with the pace of my healing.
I am patient during confusing times,
    knowing all is in divine order.
I turn inward and remember to focus on the
    task of the moment and not on the goal.
I take deep breaths whenever I lose
    patience because this slows me down
    and balances me in the moment.

*I receive patience from my Higher Self
to go through the healing process.*

Resistance

I honor the resistances I sometimes feel to going forward and to making changes.

By giving my time and attention to my resistances, they will show me where I need to place my attention in order to grow.

I do not judge or push myself before I am ready to make changes.

When my discomfort is greater than my resistance, I know I will take the needed steps towards healing.

I honor my resistances. They show me where I need to place my attention in order to grow.

Loving Myself

I practice loving myself.

I do not expect other people to unconditionally love me...they may not know how. (Remember, a person can only love you if they love themselves).

I say kind, supportive things to myself in my self-talk.

I choose to love myself when I make a mistake or someone else is displeased with me.

I feel kind and loving toward myself.

Free to Be

I am free to be my True Self.
I express this Self, and it feels good.
I continue to spend time with myself to
    calmly look inward in order to redefine
    my needs, wants, wishes, hopes, dreams,
    goals, values, and beliefs.
I am not my behavior, thoughts, and
    emotions.
I am the one who behaves, thinks, and
    feels.

I am free to be who I am.

Think

I think about why I do the things that do not
   support my growth.
Today, I study one aspect about myself that
   needs to be changed.
As I discover what the motivation is, I can
   decide rationally how I can do things
   differently.
Since I want different results, I am willing to
   think deeply about aspects of my
   character that interfere with my growth.

*I think about why I do things so I can
solve my problems.*

Boundaries

I choose to have clear boundaries.
I check in with my Inner Self when people
  want me to do something.
The better I listen to my Self, the better I can
  say "yes" or "no" to support myself.
I practice loving myself so that I will have
  the courage to risk rejection by saying
  "no" to things that are not good for me.

I have the right to say, "no,"
as well as, "yes."

Good

I know that I am good.
I know that I am at my best when my self-
esteem is high.
My intentions are to do, think, and be my
best at each moment.
This inner awareness is not dependent on
any other person's opinion.
My spiritual essence is the real me.

I know I am good.

Smiling

I smile to express my good feelings and to relate with others.
I no longer hide my joy.
I am growing in my ability to love myself.
As my feelings of worthiness grow, it automatically shows on my face.
I have a willingness to express on the outside the good feelings I am feeling on the inside.
Genuine smiles open doors when I relate to others.

I smile to express joy and to open doors of relating to others.

Laughter

I laugh at myself often.
I no longer take myself too seriously.
Laughter heals me.
When I lighten up, I make wiser choices and
    handle my mistakes easily.
Laughter helps me express feelings of
    tension and discomfort, as well as joy
    and fun.

I like to laugh at myself.

Deserving

I deserve to feel good, happy, and
 confident.
My new level of self-esteem allows me to
 have these good feelings.
I remember constantly that I am like the
 acorn growing in its perfection to the
 mighty oak.
It is never too late to grow strong branches
 that were missed earlier.

I deserve to feel good, happy,
and confident.

God Within

In the holiday season, I focus on my spiritual
    essence, or God within me.
I go within to listen to my wise Inner Self to
    move in, around, and through all the
    glamour and distractions of the
    commercial outer world.
God speaks to me when I am quiet and
    focused inward.
I take time in my busy day to center myself
    and focus within.

*I listen to God within me to help me
move in the material world.*

Winter Solstice

I go within today to experience the ending
of one cycle and the beginning of a new
one.
The quiet stillness of winter slows me down
and allows my roots of consciousness to
grow to greater depth.
I have spent almost a year focusing on
loving myself.
It is now time to rest and quietly assimilate
what has been gained.

*I go within to feel the ending of a cycle
and prepare for a new birth.*

Teacher Within

I go within to feel the quiet voice of my
    teacher within.
I ask for guidance and insight in order to live
    a fuller life.
My life purpose unfolds as I listen.
I feel a desire to take on greater
    responsibility than I had a year ago.
This past year spent learning to love myself
    from the perspective of my Higher Self
    has given me a fullness that I now want
    to share with others.
I ask my inner teacher to guide me.
I experience the Will of the Source in my life.

I will to will Thy will.

Joy

I feel the joy of the holiday season.
I feel united with the God within.
I feel centered and full.
I no longer feel the separateness from my
    spiritual nature.
I am one with all that is.
I am a channel for love to express through
    me on this earth plane.
I feel the light of day as I continue to
    awaken.
The darkness of being unconscious is behind
    me.

***I am full of joy and spread my light
to others.***

Preparation

I prepare my consciousness for the rebirth.
I spend the day in an active meditation.
Wherever I go, I am tuned into the spiritual
    essence of life.
I release negative programming from past
    experiences and interpretations of the
    holidays.
I attune myself, and I consciously connect
    with each person I meet.
I remember my wholeness and live from my
    fullness.

***I prepare my consciousness for
the new birth.***

Christ Consciousness

Today, I am a realized being having
accepted the rebirth of the higher
consciousness within my life.
The Christ within me is reborn.
I use the Christmas story to remind me of all
the parts of myself.
I am my own mother, father, and child.
I am one with the angels and wise men; all
are part of my consciousness.

*I accept the rebirth of the Christ
Consciousness within me.*

Retreat

I rest and nurture myself today.
I treat myself kindly.
I retreat to build my inner strength; I go
within and review my year.
I notice where I have improved my self-
esteem and where I still need to grow in
awareness.
I make an honest assessment of all my
behavior, thoughts, and feelings.
I write my insights in my journal.

I retreat in strength to review my year.

Future

I write a letter to myself today that I will read
in one year.

I list everything I want to experience, learn,
and accomplish in the next year.

I clarify what is practical to achieve in one
year, taking note of what may be
unrealistic desires.

This letter of intent will guide me during the
year.

If I know what the plan is, I can begin
moving forward on this path.

I make a realistic plan for my next year.

Now

I accept where I am right now on the path
of life.
By reviewing my year and planning ahead
for the next, I gently allow myself to feel
centered right now.
I release judgments of past behaviors which
I felt were not as positive as they might
have been.
I steady myself to live from this point in time
and to be realistic about the pace of my
growth.
I let go of all unrealistic expectations and
acknowledge myself for all the growth
and expansion in awareness I have
achieved.

I appreciate where I am now.

Awakening

I awaken to the awareness that I am much,
  much more than I thought.
I feel the truth about what my mind has
  been learning this past year.
I feel my spiritual wholeness and my
  connection to the greater plan and
  purpose for me as an individual as well as
  for me as a part of the greater whole.
I am a spiritual being who is waking up to
  my magnificence.

*I awaken to the splendor of my part in
the great plan of the Universe.*

Purification

I prepare myself to join others of like mind in
World Healing Day which is tomorrow.
I purify myself with proper diet, exercise,
rest, thought, and meditation.
I prepare myself to be a clear channel for
Love from the Higher Power.

At noon, Greenwich time,(7:00 a.m.
Eastern Standard Time) on
December 31, I align myself with
people all over the world by reading
the World Healing Meditation on the
next page.

*I purify myself to be a clear channel
of Love.*

World Healing Meditation

In the beginning.
In the beginning *God.*
In the beginning God created the heaven
   and the earth.
And God said Let there be light; and there
   was light.

Now is the time of the *new* beginning.
I am a co-creator with God, and it is a new
   Heaven that comes, as the Good Will of
   God is expressed on Earth through me.
It is the Kingdom of Light, Love, Peace and
   Understanding.
And I am doing my part to reveal its Reality.

I begin with me.
I am a living Soul and the Spirit of God
   dwells in me, as me.
I and the Father are one, and all that the
   Father has is mine.
In Truth, I am the Christ of God.

What is true of me is true of everyone, for
    God is all and all is God.
I see only the Spirit of God in every Soul,
    And to every man, woman and child on
    Earth I say: I love you, for you are me.
You are my Holy Self.

I now open my heart, and let the pure
    essence of Unconditional Love pour out.
I see it as a Golden Light radiating from the
    center of my being, and I feel its Divine
    Vibration in and through me, above and
    below me.

I am one with the Light.
I am filled with the Light.
I am illumined by the Light.
I am the Light of the world.

With purpose of mind, I send forth the Light.
I let the radiance go before me to join the
    other Lights.
I know this is happening all over the world at
    this moment.
I see the merging Lights.
There is now one Light.
We are the Light of the world.

The one Light of Love, Peace and
   Understanding is moving.
It flows across the face of the Earth,
   touching and illuminating every soul in
   the shadow of the illusion.
And where there was darkness, there is now
   the Light of Reality.

And the Radiance grows, permeating,
   saturating every form of life.
There is only the vibration of one Perfect Life
   now.
All the kingdoms of the Earth respond, and
   the Planet is alive with Light and Love.

There is total Oneness, and in this Oneness
   we speak the Word.
Let the sense of separation be dissolved.
Let mankind be returned to Godkind.

Let peace come forth in every mind.
Let Love flow forth from every heart.
Let forgiveness reign in every soul.
Let understanding be the common bond.

And now from the Light of the world, the
    One Presence and Power of the Universe
    responds.
The Activity of God is healing and
    harmonizing Planet Earth.
Omnipotence is made manifest.

I am seeing the salvation of the planet
    before my very eyes, as all false beliefs
    and error patterns are dissolved.
The sense of separation is no more; the
    healing has taken place, and the world is
    restored to sanity.

This is the beginning of Peace on Earth and
    Good Will toward all, as Love flows forth
    from every heart, forgiveness reigns in
    every soul, and all hearts and minds are
    one in perfect understanding.

It is done. And it is so.

For more information, read John Price's
book, *The Planetary Commission*,
available at a bookstore or from The
Quartus Foundation, P.O. Box 1768,
Boerne, Texas 78006-6768, 512/537-4689.

World Healing

I feel peace and joy for the sharing of my
   energy in the global mind link for world
   peace.
I am part of the critical mass of
   consciousness that moves humanity in a
   peaceful direction.

*I am one with all minds that join for
world healing and peace.*

C

H

I

J

N

O

P

SELF-ESTEEM BOOKS AND PRODUCTS
by Suzanne E. Harrill, M. Ed.

BOOKS
Affirm Your Self Day By Day......................$16.95
Seed Thoughts for Loving Your Self
ISBN 1-883648-22-X
Empowering You To Love Yourself..............10.95
ISBN 1-883648-01-7
You Could Feel Good....................................8.95
ISBN 0-9625996-0-3
Empowering Teens To Build Self-Esteem.....11.95
ISBN 1-883648-00-9
I Am A Star! *Children's Book*..........................7.95
ISBN 0-9625996-3-8
The I Love The Earth Book
Children's Booklet w/Colored Pencils............3.95
ISBN 0-9625996-4-6

CARDS
Adult Self-Esteem Cards 9.95
w/ Wooden Acorn
ISBN 0-9625996-5-4
Children's Self-Esteem Cards 8.95
w/ Star Eraser
ISBN 0-9625996-7-0

Seed Thoughts For Transformation
366 Affirmations from Affirm Your Self..........9.95
ISBN 0-9625996-2-X

CASSETTE
You Could Feel Good
3 Hr. Cassette Album......................................19.95
ISBN 0-9625996-6-2

FOR TEACHING
6-Week Adolescent Curriculum................89.00
Self-Esteem Curriculum Guide
For Use with 'You Could Feel Good' Book....19.95

Your Bookstore can order these self-esteem
products from these distributors : Bookpeople,
DeVorss, New Leaf or you can order from:

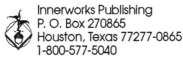 Innerworks Publishing
P. O. Box 270865
Houston, Texas 77277-0865
1-800-577-5040

Free Catalog

http://our world.compuserve.
com/home pages/innerworks

*Include $2.50 shipping for the first item and $.75 for each
additional item. Texas residents add 8.25% sales tax.*

Suzanne E. Harrill,
M. Ed., L.P.C., L.M.F.T.
Counselor, Author &
Professional Speaker

Suzanne E. Harrill is a Licensed Professional Counselor, Licensed Marriage and Family Therapist and author who has been teaching classes in self-awareness and self-esteem for over 18 years. She began her own private practice, in 1981 where she counsels individuals, couples, families and facilitates groups. Suzanne's unique and intuitive approach, along with her warmth and sense of humor, combine to provide a personal, relatable experience which facilitates and inspires people in their process of self-healing. In 1990 Suzanne began her own publishing company to publish her many works.

If you would like Suzanne to speak to your group on topics such as self-esteem, parenting, relationships or enlightened thinking, please call 713/661-8284.

Mission Statement
Innerworks Counseling & Publishing is dedicated to helping individuals and groups heal pain from the past, to know their purpose, and to reach their potential individually and collectively to make their lives count in making positive changes in the world.

The Acorn Analogy

Deep inside you know how to be you;
just as an acorn knows
how to be a mighty oak.

Remember, the acorn is doing the best it can
do at each stage of growth along its life
cycle.
It can only grow to the degree that it has
nurturing from nature: sunlight, rain water,
and nutrients from the soil.

Even if the early start was less than optimal,
the eager oak can accelerate
its desire to grow
at any time there are proper
nutrients available.

YOU ARE LIKE THE ACORN!
You, too, are doing your best under the
conditions in which you are growing.
Add a little awareness and self-acceptance
and nurturing; then watch you grow.

Nurture yourself to grow again
into your TRUE SELF, and reclaim
your birthright to feel worthy.
You deserve to be who you are.